AVON COUNTY LIBRARY

VOLUME 1

James Fenton was born in Lincoln in 1949 and educated at Magdalen College, Oxford, where he won the Newdigate Prize for Poetry. He has worked as journalist, drama critic and war correspondent and is now a columnist for the *Independent*. A collection of his pieces on major events in the Far East, entitled *All the Wrong Places*, was published by Penguin in 1990. His volumes of poetry include *Terminal Moraine*, *The Memory of War and Children in Exile* and *Out of Danger*, winner of the 1994 Whitbread Award for poetry. He is a Fellow of the Royal Society of Literature and was elected Oxford Professor of Poetry in May 1994.

Blake Morrison was born in Skipton, Yorkshire, in 1950. He is the author of two collections of poetry, *Dark Glasses* and *The Ballad of the Yorkshire Ripper*; of a children's book, *The Yellow House*; and of the award-winning autobiography *And When Did You Last See Your Father?* He has also written critical studies of the Movement and Seamus Heaney, and co-edited *The Penguin Book of Contemporary British Poetry*. He lives in London and is a staff writer for the *Independent on Sunday*.

Kit Wright was born in Kent in 1944 and educated at New College, Oxford. He has been a lecturer in English at Brock University, Ontario, the education secretary for the Poetry Society and Fellow-Commoner in the Creative Arts at Trinity College, Cambridge. He now devotes all his time to writing and is well known for his collections and anthologies for both children and adults, which include *The Bear Looked Over the Mountain*, *The Day Room*, *Bump-starting the Hearse*, *Short Afternoons*, *Hot Dog and Other Poems*, *Cat Among the Pigeons* and *Great Snakes*.

AN 1937366 X

AVON COUNTY
LIBRARY

Penguin Modern Poets

VOLUME 1

JAMES FENTON

BLAKE MORRISON

KIT WRIGHT

AVON COUNTY LIBRARY

Class No. 821.91

6/as

Alloc. AK   Suppl HE

PENGUIN BOOKS

Published by the Penguin Group
Penguin Books Ltd, 27 Wrights Lane, London w8 5tz, England
Penguin Books USA Inc., 375 Hudson Street, New York, New York 10014, USA
Penguin Books Australia Ltd, Ringwood, Victoria, Australia
Penguin Books Canada Ltd, 10 Alcorn Avenue, Toronto, Ontario, Canada m4v 3b2
Penguin Books (NZ) Ltd, 182–190 Wairau Road, Auckland 10, New Zealand

Penguin Books Ltd, Registered Offices: Harmondsworth, Middlesex, England

This selection first published 1995
10 9 8 7 6 5 4 3 2 1

Copyright © James Fenton, 1982, 1983, 1993
Copyright © Blake Morrison, 1984, 1987
Copyright © Kit Wright, 1974, 1977, 1983, 1989
All rights reserved

The moral right of the authors has been asserted

Filmset by Datix International Limited, Bungay, Suffolk
Printed in England by Clays Ltd, St Ives plc
Set in 10.5/14 pt Monophoto Garamond

Except in the United States of America, this book is sold subject
to the condition that it shall not, by way of trade or otherwise, be lent,
re-sold, hired out, or otherwise circulated without the publisher's
prior consent in any form of binding or cover other than that in
which it is published and without a similar condition including this
condition being imposed on the subsequent purchaser

Contents

Kit Wright

James Fenton

For Andrew Wood

What would the dead want from us
Watching from their cave?
Would they have us forever howling?
Would they have us rave
Or disfigure ourselves, or be strangled
Like some ancient emperor's slave?

None of my dead friends were emperors
With such exorbitant tastes
And none of them were so vengeful
As to have all their friends waste
Waste quite away in sorrow
Disfigured and defaced.

I think the dead would want us
To weep for what *they* have lost.
I think that our luck in continuing
Is what would affect them most.
But time would find them generous
And less self-engrossed.

And time would find them generous
As they used to be
And what else would they want from us
But an honoured place in our memory,
A favourite room, a hallowed chair,
Privilege and celebrity?

And so the dead might cease to grieve
And we might make amends
And there might be a pact between
Dead friends and living friends.
What our dead friends would want from us
Would be such living friends.

Wind

This is the wind, the wind in a field of corn.
Great crowds are fleeing from a major disaster
Down the long valleys, the green swaying wadis,
Down through the beautiful catastrophe of wind.

Families, tribes, nations and their livestock
Have heard something, seen something. An expectation
Or a gigantic misunderstanding has swept over the hilltop
Bending the ear of the hedgerow with stories of fire and sword

I saw a thousand years pass in two seconds.
Land was lost, languages rose and divided.
This lord went east and found safety.
His brother sought Africa and a dish of aloes.

Centuries, minutes later, one might ask
How the hilt of a sword wandered so far from the smithy.
And somewhere they will sing: 'Like chaff we were borne
In the wind.' This is the wind in a field of corn.

Out of the East

Out of the South came Famine.
Out of the West came Strife.
Out of the North came a storm cone
And out of the East came a warrior wind
And it struck you like a knife.
Out of the East there shone a sun
As the blood rose on the day
And it shone on the work of the warrior wind
And it shone on the heart
And it shone on the soul
And they called the sun – Dismay.

And it's a far cry from the jungle
To the city of Phnom Penh
And many try
And many die
Before they can see their homes again
And it's a far cry from the paddy track
To the palace of the king
And many go
Before they know
It's a far cry.
It's a war cry.
Cry for the war that can do this thing.

A foreign soldier came to me
And he gave me a gun
And he predicted victory
Before the year was done.

He taught me how to kill a man.
He taught me how to try.
But he forgot to say to me
How an honest man should die.

He taught me how to kill a man
Who was my enemy
But never how to kill a man
Who'd been a friend to me.

You fought the way a hero fights –
You had no head for fear
My friend, but you are wounded now
And I'm not allowed to leave you here

Alive.

Out of the East came Anger
And it walked a dusty road
And it stopped when it came to a river bank
And it pitched a camp
And it gazed across
To where the city stood
When
Out of the West came thunder
But it came without a sound
For it came at the speed of the warrior wind
And it fell on the heart
And it fell on the soul
And it shook the battleground

And it's a far cry from the cockpit
To the foxhole in the clay
And we were a
Coordinate
In a foreign land
Far away

And it's a far cry from the paddy track
To the palace of the king
And many try
And they ask why
It's a far cry.
It's a war cry.
Cry for the war that can do this thing.

Next year the army came for me
And I was sick and thin
And they put a weapon in our hands
And they told us we would win

And they feasted us for seven days
And they slaughtered a hundred cattle
And we sang our songs of victory
And the glory of the battle

And they sent us down the dusty roads
In the stillness of the night
And when the city heard from us
It burst in a flower of light.

The tracer bullets found us out.
The guns were never wrong
And the gunship said Regret Regret
The words of your victory song.

Out of the North came an army
And it was clad in black
And out of the South came a gun crew
With a hundred shells
And a howitzer
And we walked in black along the paddy track
When
Out of the West came napalm

And it tumbled from the blue
And it spread at the speed of the warrior wind
And it clung to the heart
And it clung to the soul
As napalm is designed to do

And it's a far cry from the fireside
To the fire that finds you there
In the foxhole
By the temple gate
The fire that finds you everywhere
And it's a far cry from the paddy track
To the palace of the king
And many try
And they ask why
It's a far cry.
It's a war cry.
Cry for the war that can do this thing.

My third year in the army
I was sixteen years old
And I had learnt enough, my friend,
To believe what I was told

And I was told that we would take
The city of Phnom Penh
And they slaughtered all the cows we had
And they feasted us again

And at last we were given river mines
And we blocked the great Mekong
And now we trained our rockets on
The landing-strip at Pochentong.

The city lay within our grasp.
We only had to wait.
We only had to hold the line
By the foxhole, by the temple gate

When
Out of the West came clusterbombs
And they burst in a hundred shards
And every shard was a new bomb
And it burst again
Upon our men
As they gasped for breath in the temple yard.
Out of the West came a new bomb
And it sucked away the air
And it sucked at the heart
And it sucked at the soul
And it found a lot of children there

And it's a far cry from the temple yard
To the map of the general staff
From the grease pen to the gasping men
To the wind that blows the soul like chaff
And it's a far cry from the paddy track
To the palace of the king
And many go
Before they know
It's a far cry.
It's a war cry.
Cry for the war that has done this thing.

A foreign soldier came to me
And he gave me a gun
And the liar spoke of victory
Before the year was done.

What would I want with victory
In the city of Phnom Penh?
Punish the city! Punish the people!
What would I want but punishment?

We have brought the king home to his palace.
We shall leave him there to weep
And we'll go back along the paddy track
For we have promises to keep.

For the promise made in the foxhole,
For the oath in the temple yard,
For the friend I killed on the battlefield
I shall make that punishment hard.

Out of the South came Famine.
Out of the West came Strife.
Out of the North came a storm cone
And out of the East came a warrior wind
And it struck you like a knife.
Out of the East there shone a sun
As the blood rose on the day
And it shone on the work of the warrior wind
And it shone on the heart
And it shone on the soul
And they called the sun Dismay, my friend,
They called the sun – Dismay.

Children in Exile

To J, T, L & S

'What I am is not important, whether I live or die –
    It is the same for me, the same for you.
What we do is important. This is what I have learnt.
    It is not what we are but what we do,'

Says a child in exile, one of a family
    Once happy in its size. Now there are four
Students of calamity, graduates of famine,
    Those whom geography condemns to war,

Who have settled here perforce in a strange country,
    Who are not even certain where they are.
They have learnt much. There is much more to learn.
    Each heart bears a diploma like a scar –

A red seal, always hot, always solid,
    Stamped with the figure of an overseer,
A lethal boy who has learnt to dispatch with a mattock,
    Who rules a village with sharp leaves and fear.

From five years of punishment for an offence
    It took America five years to commit
These victim-children have been released on parole.
    They will remember all of it.

They have found out: it is hard to escape from Cambodia,
    Hard to escape the justice of Pol Pot,
When they are called to report in dreams to their tormentors.
    One night is merciful, the next is not.

I hear a child moan in the next room and I see
    The nightmare spread like rain across his face
And his limbs twitch in some vestigial combat
    In some remembered place.

Oh let us not be condemned for what we are.
    It is enough to account for what we do.
Save us from the judge who says: You are your father's son,
    One of your father's crimes – your crime is you.

And save us too from that fatal geography
    Where vengeance is impossible to halt.
And save Cambodia from threatened extinction.
    Let not its history be made its fault.

They feared these woods, feared tigers, snakes and malaria.
    They thought the landscape terrible and wild.
There were ghosts under the beds in the tower room.
    A hooting owl foretold a still-born child.

And how would they survive the snows of Italy?
    For the first weeks, impervious to relief,
They huddled in dark rooms and feared the open air,
    Caught in the tight security of grief.

Fear attacked the skin and made the feet swell
    Though they were bathed in tamarind at night.
Fear would descend like a swarm of flying ants.
    It was impossible to fight.

I saw him once, doubled in pain, scratching his legs,
    This was in Pisa at the Leaning Tower.
We climbed to the next floor and his attackers vanished
    As fast as they had come. He thought some power

Some influence lurked in certain rooms and corners.
    But why was I not suffering as well?
He trod cautiously over the dead in the Campo Santo
    And saw the fading punishments of Hell

And asked whether it is true that the unjust will be tormented
    And whether those who suffer will be saved.
There are so many martyrdoms in the beautiful galleries.
    He was a connoisseur among the graves.

It was the first warm day of the year. The university
    Gossiped in friendly groups around the square.
He envied the students their marvellous education,
    Greedy for school, frantic to be in there.

On the second train he was relaxed and excited.
    For the first time he was returning home,
Pointing his pocket camera at the bright infinity of mountains.
    The winter vines shimmered like chromosomes,

Meaningless to him. The vines grew. The sap returned.
    The land became familiar and green.
The brave bird-life of Italy began planning families.
    It was the season of the selfish gene.

Lovers in cars defied the mad gynaecologist.
    In shady lanes, and later than they should,
They were watching the fireflies' brilliant use of the hyphen
    And the long dash in the darkening wood.

And then they seemed to check the car's suspension
    Or test the maximum back-axle load.
I love this valley, but I often wonder why
    There's always one bend extra in the road.

And what do the dogs defend behind the high wire fences?
    What home needs fury on a running lead?
Why did the Prince require those yellow walls?
    These private landscapes must be wealth indeed.

But you, I am glad to say, are not so fortified.
    The land just peters out behind the house.
(Although, the first time the hunters came blazing through the
                                                garden,
    Someone screamed at me: 'Get out there. What are you, mar
                                                or mouse?

When Duschko went mad and ate all those chickens
    It was a cry for help. Now he breaks loose
And visits his fellow guards, and laughs at their misery –
    Unhappy dog! So sensitive to abuse.

He thought there was a quantum of love and attention
    Which now he would be forced to share around
As first three Vietnamese and then four Cambodians
    Trespassed on his ground.

It doesn't work like that. It never has done.
    Love is accommodating. It makes space.
When they were requested to abandon their home in the haylo
    Even the doves retired with better grace.

They had the tower still, with its commanding eyelets.
    The tiles were fond of them, the sky grew kind.
They watched a new provider spreading corn on the zinc tray
    And didn't mind.

Boat people, foot people, wonky Yankee publishers –
    They'd seen the lot. They knew who slept in which beds.
They swooped down to breakfast after a night on the tiles
    And dropped a benediction on your heads.

And now the school bus comes honking through the valley
   And education litters every room –
Grammars, vocabularies, the Khao-i-Dang hedge dictionary,
   The future perfect, subjunctive moods and gloom.

So many questions in urgent need of answer:
   What is a Pope? What is a proper noun?
Where is Milan? Who won the Second World War?
   How many fluid ounces in a pound?

La Normandie est renommée par ses falaises et ses fromages.
   What are Normandy, cliffs, cheeses and fame?
Too many words on the look-out for too many meanings.
   Too many syllables for the tongue to frame.

A tiny philosopher climbs onto my knee
   And sinks his loving teeth into my arm.
He has had a good dream. A friendly gun-toting Jesus
   Has spent the night protecting him from harm.

He goes for Technical Lego and significant distinctions.
   Suppose, he says, I have a house and car,
Money and everything, I could lose it all,
   As we lost all our property in the war.

But if I have knowledge, if I know five languages,
   If I have mathematics and the rest,
No one can steal that from me. The difference is:
   No one inherits what I once possessed.

When I die, my education dies with me.
   I cannot leave my knowledge to my son,
Says this boy in exile, and he shrugs and laughs shortly.
   Whoever dreamt of Jesus with a gun?

His brother dreams all night of broken chords
  And all the summer long his broken hand,
Still calloused from hard labour, figures out a prelude.
  Music and maths are what he understands.

These dreams are messages. One of the dead sisters
  Says to the girl: 'Do not be sad for me.
I am alive and in your twin sister's womb
  In California, as you shall see.'

Some time later, the postman brings a letter from America.
  The child bride is expecting her first child.
Months afterwards, a photograph of a little girl.
  Something is reconciled.

Alone in the tower room, the twin keeps up her dancing.
  For the millionth time, Beethoven's *Für Elise*!
Little Vietnam borrows little Cambodia's toys.
  Mother America is the appeaser.

Pretending to work, I retire to the study
  And find a copy of *The Dyer's Hand*
Where I read: 'An emigrant never knows what he wants,
  Only what he does not want.' I understand

What it is I have seen, how simple and how powerful
  This flight, this negative ambition is
And how a girl in exile can gaze down into an olive grove
  And wonder: 'Is America like this?'

For it is we, not they, who cannot forgive America,
  And it is we who travel, they who flee,
We who may choose exile, they who are forced out,
  Take to the hot roads, take to the sea,

In dangerous camps between facing armies,
    The prey of pirates, raped, plundered or drowned,
In treacherous waters, in single file through the minefields,
    Praying to stave off death till they are found,

Begging for sponsors, begging for a Third Country,
    Begging America to take them in –
It is they, it is they who put everything in hazard.
    What we do decides whether they sink or swim.

Do they know what they want? They know what they do not
                                                        want.
    Better the owl before dawn than the devil by day.
Better strange food than famine, hard speech than mad labour.
    Better this quietness than that dismay.

Better ghosts under the bed than to sleep in the paddy.
    Better this frost, this blizzard than that sky.
Better a concert pianist than a corpse, an engineer than a shadow.
    Better to dance under the fresco than to die.

Better a new god with bleeding hands and feet,
    Better the painted tortures of the blest
Than the sharp leaf at the throat, the raised mattock
    And all the rest.

My dear American friends, I can't say how much it means to me
    To see this little family unfurl,
To see them relax and learn, and learn about happiness,
    The mother growing strong, the boys adept, the girl

Confident in your care. They can never forget the past.
    Let them remember, but let them not fear.
Let them find their future is delightfully accomplished
    And find perhaps America is here.

Let them come to the crest of the road when the morning is fin
    With Florence spread like honey on the plain,
Let them walk through the ghostless woods, let the guns be
                                        silent,
    The tiger never catch their eye again.

They are thriving I see. I hope they always thrive
    Whether in Italy, England or France.
Let them dream as they wish to dream. Let them dream

Of Jesus, America, maths, Lego, music and dance.

Blood and Lead

Listen to what they did.
Don't listen to what they said.
What was written in blood
Has been set up in lead.

Lead tears the heart.
Lead tears the brain.
What was written in blood
Has been set up again.

The heart is a drum.
The drum has a snare.
The snare is in the blood.
The blood is in the air.

Listen to what they did.
Listen to what's to come.
Listen to the blood.
Listen to the drum.

Jerusalem

1

Stone cries to stone,
Heart to heart, heart to stone,
And the interrogation will not die
For there is no eternal city
And there is no pity
And there is nothing underneath the sky
No rainbow and no guarantee –
There is no covenant between your God and me.

2

It is superb in the air.
Suffering is everywhere
And each man wears his suffering like a skin.
My history is proud.
Mine is not allowed.
This is the cistern where all wars begin,
The laughter from the armoured car.
This is the man who won't believe you're what you are.

3

This is your fault.
This is a crusader vault.
The Brook of Kidron flows from Mea She'arim.
I will pray for you.
I will tell you what to do.
I'll stone you. I shall break your every limb.
Oh I am not afraid of you
But maybe I should fear the things you make me do.

4

    This is not Golgotha.
    This is the Holy Sepulchre,
  The Emperor Hadrian's temple to a love
    Which he did not much share.
    Golgotha could be anywhere.
Jerusalem itself is on the move.
    It leaps and leaps from hill to hill
And as it makes its way it also makes its will.

5

    The city was sacked.
    Jordan was driven back.
  The pious Christians burned the Jews alive.
    This is a minaret.
    I'm not finished yet.
We're waiting for reinforcements to arrive.
    What was your mother's real name?
Would it be safe today to go to Bethlehem?

6

    This is the Garden Tomb.
    No, *this* is the Garden Tomb.
  I'm an Armenian. I am a Copt.
    This is Utopia.
    I came here from Ethiopia.
This hole is where the flying carpet dropped
    The Prophet off to pray one night
And from here one hour later he resumed his flight.

7

Who packed your bag?
I packed my bag.
Where was your uncle's mother's sister born?
Have you ever met an Arab?
Yes I am a scarab.
I am a worm. I am a thing of scorn.
I cry Impure from street to street
And see my degradation in the eyes I meet.

8

I am your enemy.
This is Gethsemane.
The broken graves look to the Temple Mount.
Tell me now, tell me when
When shall we all rise again?
Shall I be first in that great body count?
When shall the tribes be gathered in?
When, tell me, when shall the Last Things begin?

9

You are in error.
This is terror.
This is your banishment. This land is mine.
This is what you earn.
This is the Law of No Return.
This is the sour dough, this the sweet wine.
This is my history, this my race
And this unhappy man threw acid in my face.

Stone cries to stone,
Heart to heart, heart to stone.
These are the warrior archaeologists.
This is us and that is them.
This is Jerusalem.
These are the dying men with tattooed wrists.
Do this and I'll destroy your home.
I have destroyed your home. You have destroyed my home.

December 1988

The Milkfish Gatherers

To G.L.

The sea sounds insincere
Giving and taking with one hand.
It stopped a river here last month
Filling its mouth with sand.

They drag the shallows for the milkfish fry –
Two eyes on a glass noodle, nothing more.
Roused by his vigilant young wife
The drowsy stevedore.

Comes running barefoot past the swamp
To meet a load of wood.
The yellow peaked cap, the patched pink shorts
Seem to be all his worldly goods.

The nipa booths along the coast
Protect the milkfish gatherers' rights.
Nothing goes unobserved. My good custodian
Sprawls in the deckchair through the night.

Take care, he says, take care –
Not everybody is a friend.
And so he makes my life more private still –
A privacy on which he will attend.

But the dogs are sly with the garbage
And the cats ruthless, even with sliced bread,
As the terns are ruthless among the shoals.
Men watch the terns, then give the boat its head

Dragging a wide arc through the blue,
Trailing their lines,
Cutting the engine out
At the first sign.

A hundred feet away
Something of value struggles not to die.
It will sell for a dollar a kilo.
It weighs two kilos on the line – a prize.

And the hull fills with a fortune
And the improbable colours of the sea
But the spine lives when the brain dies
In a convulsive misery.

Rummagers of inlets, scourers of the deep,
Dynamite men, their bottles crammed with wicks,
They named the sea's inhabitants with style –
The slapped vagina fish, the horse's dick.

Polillo 'melts' means it is far away –
The smoking island plumed from slash and burn.
And from its shore, busy with hermit crabs,
Look to Luzon. Infanta melts in turn.

The setting sun behind the Sierra Madre
Projects a sharp blue line across the sky
And in the eastern glow beyond Polillo
It looks as if another sun might rise –

As if there were no night,
Only a brother evening and a dawn.
No night! No death! How could these people live?
How could the pressure lanterns lure the prawns?

Nothing of value has arrived all day –
No timber, no rattan. Now after dark,
The news comes from the sea. They crowd the beach
And prime a lantern, waiting for the shark.

The young receive the gills, which they will cook.
The massive liver wallows on the shore
And the shark's teeth look like a row of sharks
Advancing along a jaw.

Alone again by spirit light
I notice something happening on a post.
Something has burst its skin and now it hangs,
Hangs for dear life onto its fine brown ghost.

Clinging exhausted to its former self,
Its head flung back as if to watch the moon,
The blue-green veins pulsing along its wings,
The thing unwraps itself, but falls too soon.

The ants are tiny and their work is swift –
The insect-shark is washed up on their land –
While the sea sounds insincere,
Giving and taking with one hand.

At dawn along the seashore come
The milkfish gatherers, human fry.
A white polythene bowl
Is what you need to sort the milkfish by.

For a hatched fish is a pair of eyes –
There is nothing more to see.
But the spine lives when the brain dies
In a convulsive misery.

The Ballad of the Shrieking Man

A shrieking man stood in the square
And he harangued the smart café
In which a bowlered codger sat
A-twirling of a fine moustache
A-drinking of a fine Tokay

And it was Monday and the town
Was working in a kind of peace
Excepting where the shrieking man
A-waving of his tattered limbs
Glared at the codger's trouser-crease

Saying

Coffee's mad
And tea is mad
And so are gums and teeth and lips.
The horror ships that ply the seas
The horror tongues that plough the teeth
The coat
The tie
The trouser clips
The purple sergeant with the bugger-grips
Will string you up with all their art
And laugh their socks off as you blow apart.

The codger seeming not to hear
Winked at the waiter, paid the bill
And walked the main street out of town
Beyond the school, beyond the works
Where the shrieking man pursued him still

And there the town beneath them lay
And there the desperate river ran.
The codger smiled a purple smile.
A finger sliced his waistcoat ope
And he rounded on the shrieking man

Saying

Tramps are mad
And truth is mad
And so are trees and trunks and tracks.
The horror maps have played us true.
The horror moon that slits the clouds
The gun
The goon
The burlap sacks
The purple waistcoats of the natterjacks
Have done their bit as you can see
To prise the madness from our sanity.

On Wednesday when the day was young
Two shrieking men came into town
And stopped before the smart café
In which another codger sat
Twirling his whiskers with a frown

And as they shrieked and slapped their knees
The codger's toes began to prance
Within the stitching of their caps
Which opened like a set of jaws
And forced him out to join the dance.

Saying

Arms are mad
And legs are mad

And all the spaces in between.
The horror spleen that bursts its sack
The horror purple as it lunges through
The lung
The bung
The jumping-bean
The I-think-you-know-what-you-think-I-mean
Are up in arms against the state
And all the body will disintegrate.

On Saturday the town was full
As people strolled in seeming peace
Until three shrieking men appeared
And danced before the smart café
And laughed and jeered and slapped their knees

And there a hundred codgers sat.
A hundred adam's apples rose
And rubbed against their collar studs
Until the music came in thuds
And all the men were on their toes

Saying

Hearts are mad
And minds are mad
And bats are moons and moons are bats.
The horror cats that leap the tiles
The horror slates that catch the wind
The lice
The meat
The burning ghats
The children buried in the butter vats
The steeple crashing through the bedroom roof
Will be your answer if you need a proof.

The codgers poured into the square
And soon their song was on all lips
And all did dance and slap their knees
Until a horseman came in view –
The sergeant with the bugger-grips!

He drew his cutlass, held it high
And brought it down on hand and head
And ears were lopped and limbs were chopped
And still the sergeant slashed and slew
Until the codger crew lay dead

Saying

God is mad
And I am mad
And I am God and you are me.
The horror peace that boils the sight
The horror God turning out the light.
The Christ
Who killed
The medlar tree
Is planning much the same for you and me
And here's a taste of what's in store –
Come back again if you should want some more.

On Sunday as they hosed the streets
I went as usual to pray
And cooled my fingers at the stoup
And when the wafer touched my tongue
I thought about that fine Tokay

And so I crossed the empty square
And met the waiter with a wink
A-sweeping up of severed heads
A-piling up of bowler hats
And he muttered as he poured my drink

Saying

Waiting's mad
And stating's mad
And understating's mad as hell.
The undertakings we have made
The wonder breaking from the sky
The pin
The pen
The poisoned well
The purple sergeant with the nitrate smell
Have won their way and while we wait
The horror ships have passed the straits—
The vice
The vine
The strangler fig
The fault of thinking small and acting big
Have primed the bomb and pulled the pin
And we're all together when the roof falls in!

Cut-Throat Christ

or the New Ballad of the Dosi Pares

Oh the Emperor sat on an ivory throne
And his wives were fat and all their jewels shone
And the Emperor said: It's plain to see
Christ was an emperor just like me.

Well the rich have a Christ and he's nobody's fool
And he pays for their kids to go to convent school
And their momma drives them home to tea.
She says: Christ is a rich bitch just like me.

But *I* say:

I say he sold his body to some foreign queer
And he sold his blood for just a case of beer
And he sold his soul to the fraternity.
Christ became a cut-throat just like me.

There's a Christ for a whore and a Christ for a punk
A Christ for a pickpocket and a drunk
There's a Christ for every sinner but one thing there aint –
There aint no Christ for any cutprice saint.

Well I was casting for fish by the North Harbour Pier
When this guy called Jesus says to me: Come here –
If you want to join the fraternity,
Lay down your nets and you can follow me.

So I left my nets and I left my line
And I followed my Jesus to the Quiapo shrine
And he told me many stories of his enemy –
It was General Ching of the EPD.

And I swore to the Black Nazarene there and then
I'd go out and kill one of the General's men
And when I brought my *beinte-nuebe* for the boss to see
That guy called Jesus he was proud of me.

Oh the Emperor sat on an ivory throne.
He had twelve brave peers and he loved each one.
We were twelve disciples and our strength was proved
But I was the disciple whom Jesus loved.

There's a Christ for a whore and a Christ for a punk
A Christ for a pickpocket and a drunk
There's a Christ for every sinner but one thing there aint —
There aint no Christ for any cutprice saint.

Well Jesus was a drinker as you might expect.
We got through plenty stainless and a few long necks
And then Jesus got mad as mad can be.
He said: One of you punks is gonna squeal on me.

Now that General Ching has put a price on my head
With disciples like you I'm as good as dead —
There's one who will betray me to the EPD.
We said: Tell me boss, tell me boss, is it me?

But there wasn't the leisure and there wasn't the time
To find out from Jesus who would do this crime
For a shot rang out and we had to flee
From General Ching and half the military.

Oh the Emperor sat on an ivory throne
And out of twelve brave peers there was just one bad one
And Christ had twelve disciples and they loved him so
But one out of twelve is just the way things go.

There's a Christ for a whore and a Christ for a punk
A Christ for a pickpocket and a drunk
There's a Christ for every sinner but one thing there aint —
There aint no Christ for any cutprice saint.

Well I ran like crazy and I ran like fuck
And for the next three days I did my best to duck
And then I made my way back to the EPD.
I said: The General said he had a job for me.

Well the General he saw me and his face grew grim.
He said: Watch it guys, don't stand too close to him —
That's our old friend Judas and he wants his fee,
But the guy called Jesus he is roaming free.

I said: What's the deal? He said: We killed him, sure,
We filled him full of what we had and then some more,
We dumped him back in Tondo for his momma to see
And now he's resurrected with a one, two, three.

I said: General Ching, if what you say is true
I'm gonna need some protection out of you.
He said: Just pay him off now and let me be —
We don't protect a mediocrity.

'Cos the Emperor sat on an ivory throne
But that was long ago and now the Emperor's gone
And this guy called Jesus he is something new:
You crucify him once and he comes back for you.

We've dumped him in the Pasig, we've thrown him in the
                                                    Bay,
We've nixed him in the cogon by the Superhighway,
We've chopped him into pieces and we've spread him
                                                around
But three days later he is safe and he is sound.

34

There's a Christ for a whore and a Christ for a punk
A Christ for a pickpocket and a drunk
There's a Christ for every sinner but one thing there aint —
There aint no Christ for any cutprice saint.

Now Manila's not the place for a defenceless thing —
You either go with Jesus or with General Ching
And I'd been with both and after what I'd been
I knew my only hope was the Black Nazarene.

So I go barefoot down to Quiapo and the streets are
                                                    packed
And they're carrying the Nazarene on their backs
And just one step and it's plain to see
That Christ will crush them to eternity —

The Christ of the Aztecs, the Juggernaut God,
The Christ of the Thorn and the Christ of the Rod
And they're carrying the Christ along two lengths of rope
'Cos the Cut-Throat Christ's a cut-throat's only hope

And there's the man who killed the Carmelites, the
                                                    Tad-tad gang,
The man who sells the Armalites in Alabang
And General Ching, the EPD, the senatorial bets,
The twelve disciples and the drum majorettes,

The Emperor Charlemagne, the rich bitch and the queer,
The guy called Jesus by the North Harbour Pier
And they're coming down to Quiapo and they've all made
                                                    a vow
To wipe the sweat from the Black Nazarene's brow.

Oh the Emperor sat on an ivory throne
But in a cut-throat world a man is on his own
And what I've got is what you see –
Cut-Throat Christ, don't turn your back on me.

The *dosi pares* are the Twelve Peers of Charlemagne, whose legend was retailed in the old Tagalog ballads. Today the term *dosi pares* is often used to indicate a criminal gang, both in Manila and in the provinces. A *beinte-nuebe* is a kind of butterfly knife, so called after its 29-centimetre blade. 'Stainless' is a kind of gin, a 'long neck' refers to any 75 centilitre bottle of spirits. The statue of the Black Nazarene is to be found in the Quiapo church in the market area of downtown Manila. Of seventeenth-century origin and Aztec workmanship, it is the object of a widespread cult particularly among members of the underworld.

The Mistake

With the mistake your life goes in reverse.
Now you can see exactly what you did
Wrong yesterday and wrong the day before
And each mistake leads back to something worse

And every nuance of your hypocrisy
Towards yourself, and every excuse
Stands solidly on the perspective lines
And there is perfect visibility.

What an enlightenment. The colonnade
Rolls past on either side. You needn't move.
The statues of your errors brush your sleeve.
You watch the tale turn back – and you're dismayed.

And this dismay at this, this big mistake
Is made worse by the sight of all those who
Knew all along where these mistakes would lead –
Those frozen friends who watched the crisis break.

Why didn't they *say*? Oh, but they did indeed –
Said with a murmur when the time was wrong
Or by a mild refusal to assent
Or told you plainly but you would not heed.

Yes, you can hear them now. It hurts. It's worse
Than any sneer from any enemy.
Take this dismay. Lay claim to this mistake.
Look straight along the lines of this reverse.

Out of Danger

Heart be kind and sign the release
As the trees their loss approve.
Learn as leaves must learn to fall
Out of danger, out of love.

What belongs to frost and thaw
Sullen winter will not harm.
What belongs to wind and rain
Is out of danger from the storm.

Jealous passion, cruel need
Betray the heart they feed upon.
But what belongs to earth and death
Is out of danger from the sun.

I was cruel, I was wrong –
Hard to say and hard to know.
You do not belong to me.
You are out of danger now –

Out of danger from the wind,
Out of danger from the wave,
Out of danger from the heart
Falling, falling out of love.

The Skip

I took my life and threw it on the skip,
Reckoning the next-door neighbours wouldn't mind
If my life hitched a lift to the council tip
With their dry rot and rubble. What you find

With skips is – the whole community joins in.
Old mattresses appear, doors kind of drift
Along with all that won't fit in the bin
And what the bin-men can't be fished to shift.

I threw away my life, and there it lay
And grew quite sodden. 'What a dreadful shame,'
Clucked some old bag and sucked her teeth: 'The way
The young these days . . . no values . . . me, I blame . . .'

But I blamed no one. Quality control
Had loused it up, and that was that. 'Nough said.
I couldn't stick at home. I took a stroll
And passed the skip, and left my life for dead.

Without my life, the beer was just as foul,
The landlord still as filthy as his wife,
The chicken in the basket was an owl,
And no one said: 'Ee, Jim-lad, whur's thee life?'

Well, I got back that night the worse for wear,
But still just capable of single vision;
Looked in the skip; my life – it wasn't there!
Some bugger'd nicked it – *without* my permission.

Okay, so I got angry and began
To shout, and woke the street. Okay. *Okay!*
And I was sick all down the neighbour's van.
And I disgraced myself on the par-*kay*.

And then . . . you know how if you've had a few
You'll wake at dawn, all healthy, like sea breezes,
Raring to go, and thinking: 'Clever you!
You've got away with it.' And then, oh Jesus,

It hits you. Well, that morning, just at six
I woke, got up and looked down at the skip.
There lay my life, still sodden, on the bricks;
There lay my poor old life, arse over tip.

Or was it mine? Still dressed, I went downstairs
And took a long cool look. The truth was dawning.
Someone had just exchanged my life for theirs.
Poor fool, I thought – I should have left a warning.

Some bastard saw my life and thought it nicer
Than what he had. Yet what he'd had seemed fine.
He'd never caught his fingers in the slicer
The way I'd managed in that life of mine.

His life lay glistening in the rain, neglected,
Yet still a decent, an authentic life.
Some people I can think of, I reflected
Would take that thing as soon as you'd say Knife.

It seemed a shame to miss a chance like that.
I brought the life in, dried it by the stove.
It looked so fetching, stretched out on the mat.
I tried it on. It fitted, like a glove.

And now, when some local bat drops off the twig
And new folk take the house, and pull up floors
And knock down walls and hire some kind of big
Container (say, a skip) for their old doors,

I'll watch it like a hawk, and every day
I'll make at least – oh – half a dozen trips.
I've furnished an existence in that way.
You'd not believe the things you find on skips.

I'll Explain

It's something you say at your peril.
It's something you shouldn't contain.
It's a truth for the dark and a pillow.
Turn out the light and I'll explain.

It's the obvious truth of the morning
Bitten back as the sun turns to rain,
To the rain, to the dark, to the pillow.
Turn out the light and I'll explain.

> It's what I was hoping to tell you.
> It's what I was hoping you'd guess.
> It's what I was hoping you *wouldn't* guess
> Or you wouldn't mind.
> It's a kind
> Of hopelessness.

It's the hope that you hope at your peril.
It's the hope that you fear to attain.
It's the obvious truth of the evening.
Turn out the light and I'll explain.

The Possibility

The lizard on the wall, engrossed,
The sudden silence from the wood
Are telling me that I have lost
The possibility of good.

I know this flower is beautiful
And yesterday it seemed to be.
It opened like a crimson hand.
It was not beautiful to me.

I know that work is beautiful.
It is a boon. It is a good.
Unless my working were a way
Of squandering my solitude.

And solitude was beautiful
When I was sure that I was strong.
I thought it was a medium
In which to grow, but I was wrong.

The jays are swearing in the wood.
The lizard moves with ugly speed.
The flower closes like a fist.
The possibility recedes.

Hinterhof

Stay near to me and I'll stay near to you —
As near as you are dear to me will do,
    Near as the rainbow to the rain,
    The west wind to the windowpane,
As fire to the hearth, as dawn to dew.

Stay true to me and I'll stay true to you —
As true as you are new to me will do,
    New as the rainbow in the spray,
    Utterly new in every way,
New in the way that what you say is true.

Stay near to me, stay true to me. I'll stay
As near, as true to you as heart could pray.
    Heart never hoped that one might be
    Half of the things you are to me —
The dawn, the fire, the rainbow and the day.

Here Come the Drum Majorettes!

There's a girl with a fist full of fingers.
There's a man with a fist full of fivers.
There's a thrill in a step as it lingers.
There's a chance for a pair of salivas —

For the

Same hat
Same shoes
Same giddy widow on a sunshine cruise
Same deck
Same time
Same disappointment in a gin-and-lime

It's the same chalk on the blackboard!
It's the same cheese on the sideboard!
It's the same cat on the boardwalk!
It's the same broad on the catwalk!

There's a Gleb on a steppe in a dacha.
There's a Glob on a dig on the slack side.
There's a Glubb in the sand (he's a pasha).
There's a glib gammaglob in your backside

Saying

Gleb meet Glubb.
Glubb meet Glob.
God that's glum, that glib Glob dig.
'Dig that bog!'
'Frag that frog.'
'Stap that chap, he snuck that cig.'

45

It's the same ice on the race-track!
It's the same track through the pack-ice!
It's the same brick in the ice-pack!
It's the same trick with an ice-pick!

There's a thing you can pull with your eyeballs.
There's a tin you can pour for a bullshot.
There's a can you can shoot for a bullseye.
There's a man you can score who's an eyesore.

I'm an
Eyesore.
You're the thing itself.
You've a
Price or
You'd be on the shelf.
I'm a loner
In a lonesome town –
Barcelona –
It can get you down.

It's the same scare with a crowbar!
It's the same crow on the barstool!
It's the same stool for the scarecrow!
It's the same bar!

Ho!

Ha!

Like a spark from the stack of a liner
Like a twig in the hands of a dowser
With the force of the fist of a miner
(With the grace and the speed of a trouser)

In a

Blue moon
In a blue lagoon
She's got blue blue bloomers in a blue monsoon.

Wearing blue boots
And a blue zoot suit
He's a cruising bruiser with a shooter and a cute little
Twin blade
Sin trade
In a
Blue brown
New Town.

It's the same hand on the windpipe!
It's the same sand in the windsock!
It's the same brand on the handbag!
It's the same gland in the handjob!

The room is black.
The knuckles crack.
The blind masseuse walks up your back.
The saxophone
Is on its own
Pouring out the *Côtes du Rhône*.

When you're down to your last pair of piastres.
When you're down on your luck down in Przemyśl,
When your life is a chain of disasters
And your death you believe would be sameish,

When the goat has gone off with the gander
Or the goose with the grebe or the grouper
Then – a drum majorette – you can stand her:
She's a brick – she's a gas – she's a trouper

Saying

Jane meet John.
John meet Jane.
Take those jimjams off again
Jezebel.
Just as well.
Join the jive with Jules and June.
Geoffrey, Jesus, Jason, Jim,
Jenny, Jilly, Golly Gee –
If it's the same for you and him
It's the same for you and me:

It's the same grin on the loanshark!
It's the same goon in the sharkskin!
It's the same shark in the skin-game!
It's the same game
Same same

It's the same old rope for to skip with!
It's the same Old Nick for to sup with
    With a long spoon
    To the wrong tune

And it's hard for a heart to put up with!

Blake Morrison

Xerox

They come each evening like virgins to a well:
the girls queuing for the Xerox-machine,
braceleted and earmarked, shapely as pitchers
in their stretch Levis or wraparound shirts,
sylphs from the typing pool bearing the forms
of their masters, the chilly boardroom gods.

But this one, this nervous one, is different.
She doesn't gossip with the others and pleads,
when it's her turn, *no, you go first*.
Not until they've gone, their anklets chinking
down the corridor, does she lift the hatch
and dip her trembling hand into the well.

A lightshow begins under the trapdoor:
it flashes and roars, flashes and plashes,
each page the flare of a sabotaged refinery
or the fission of an August storm.
Minutes pass, they slide into the wastebin,
but something is committed for all time.

Sweet-faced, two-faced, a face for every paper,
you were never so alone again.
They took a week or more to find you,
but they found you, posseed to the courtroom
under a scarlet rug, cheeks lit palely
in the lightning of a Nikon swarm.

And what has this to do with it? How you stood
one night by a heifers' drinking-trough
near Yelverton, afraid and down-at-heel
in a mud-churned, midge-drizzling negative,
then saw the country rising from its shadow
under the sudden candour of a moon.

The Kiss

His Buick was too wide and didn't slow,
our wing-mirrors kissing in a Suffolk lane,
no sweat, not worth the exchange of addresses.

High from the rainchecking satellites
our island's like a gun set on a table,
still smoking, waiting to be loaded again.

On Sizewell Beach

There are four beach huts, numbered 13 to 16,
each with net curtains and a lock.
Who owns them, what happened to the first twelve,
whether there are plans for further building:
there's no one here today to help with such inquiries,
the café closed up for the winter,
no cars or buses in the PAY AND DISPLAY.
The offshore rig is like a titan's diving board.
I've heard the rumours that it's warmer here
for bathing than at any other point along the coast.
Who started them? The same joker who bought
the village pub and named it the Vulcan,
'God of fire and metalwork and hammers,
deformed and buffoonish, a forger of rich thrones'?
Whoever he is, whatever he was up to,
he'd be doused today, like these men out back,
shooting at clay pigeons, the rain in their Adnams beer.
And now a movement on the shingle
that's more than the scissoring of terns:
a fishing boat's landed, three men in yellow waders
guiding it shorewards over metal-ribbed slats
which they lay in front of it like offerings
while the winch in its hut, tense and oily,
hauls at the hook in the prow, the smack with its catch
itself become a catch, though when I lift
the children up to see the lockjaws of sole and whiting
there's nothing in there but oilskin and rope.

I love this place, its going on with life
in the shadow of the slab behind it,
which you almost forget, or might take for a giant's Lego
    set,
so neat are the pipes and the chain-mail fences,
the dinky railway track running off to Leiston,
the pylons like a line of cross-country skiers,
the cooling ponds and turbine halls and reactor control
    rooms
where they prove with geigers on Open Days
('Adults and Children over 14 years only')
that sealed plutonium is less radioactive than a watch.

One rain-glossed Saturday in April
a lad from Halesworth having passed his test
and wanting to impress his girlfriend
came here in the Ford he'd borrowed from his father
and took the corner much too fast, too green to judge
the danger or simply not seeing the child
left on the pavement by the father – no less reckless –
who had crossed back to his Renault for the notebook
he'd stupidly forgotten, the one with jottings
for a poem about nuclear catastrophe,
a poem later abandoned, in place of which
he'd write of the shock of turning round
to find a car had come between him and his daughter,
an eternity of bodywork blotting out the view,
a cloud or an eclipse which hangs before the eyes
and darkens all behind them, clearing at last
to the joy of finding her still standing there,
the three of us spared that other life we dream of
where the worst has already happened
and we are made to dwell forever on its shore.

Grange Boy

Horse-chestnuts thudded to the lawn each autumn.
Their spiked husks were like medieval clubs,
Porcupines, unexploded mines. But if
You waited long enough they gave themselves up –
Brown pups, a cow opening its sad eye,
The shine of the dining-room table.

We were famous for horse-chestnuts. Boys
From the milltown would ring at our door asking
Could they gather conkers and I'd to tell them
Only from the ground – no stick-throwing.
I watched from the casement as they wandered
In shadow, trousers crammed like mint-jars.

One morning they began without asking.
Plain as pikestaffs, their hurled sticks filleted
Whole branches, the air filled like a pillowfight
With rebellion and leaves. I was alone.
I had not father's booming voice. They were free
To trample through our peaceable estate.

Afterwards, matching father in a show
Of indignation (*bloody vandals and thugs*),
I imagined their home ground: the flagged backyards,
The forbidden ginnels and passages
Winding up and out on purple moor,
The coal-sacks glistening in locked sheds.

It is June now, the chestnut scattered
Like confetti. He summoned me today
To the billiard-room – that incident
With an apprentice. *I've told you before.*
A son in your father's firm, you're looked to
For an example. I don't know what to do.

So I sit at my rosewood desk, lines fading
Across the parkland. I've been getting pamphlets
In a plain brown envelope and feel like
A traitor. Strangers have been seen
By the wicket-gate. Mother keeps to her bed.
English, we hoard our secrets to the end.

The Renunciation

Our lives were wasted but we never knew.
There was such work to be done: the watch-chains
And factories, the papers to sign
In the study. Surrounded by brass
How could we see what we amounted to —
A glint of eyes as headlights swept away?

In a cot on the lawn lies my nephew,
Whose name I can't remember – the strands
Of family thinner each year, though we
Are here again, politely. The sun comes through
Like a faint reminder of things not done:
Forgotten dates, brothers not loved enough.

Peter, Jenny's husband, never forgave her.
When he caught them, out by the links, it was
All quite tame – some shouts and blows, Jenny
In tears, and the lover not showing again.
But later – well, Pete really cracked. Jen said he used
The affair as a way of opting out of things for good.

Here, on this stone, a relief map of lichen,
Each mossy headland like a lush green future.
Swallows gather on the wire, darkening
The air with their forked legends – journeys
We planned to take too, had the time been right
And the distance to the airport less far.

Every verse is a last verse, concluding
Sadness. You hear its tone in the chestnuts
And rookery – how much has been taken.
The garden with its nightshade nags like some
Vague guilt and the rooms look so untidy,
But there is nothing we know of to be done.

Simon has a sperm count of ten million –
Almost no chance at all, the clinic said.
'Funny those years of worrying if the girl . . .
When all the time . . . And now Louise, who'd set
Her heart on three at least . . . there's fostering, true, but . . .
I've lost the urge as well – know what I mean.'

I have learnt lately to admire the traits
Of those who dispossess me: their scars,
Their way of getting straight to the point,
Things mattering. Their families roam the orchards,
At home among the tennis courts and lupins.
I watch – I have resigned myself to light.

Our lives run down like lawns to a sundial
And unborn children play in a world I imagine
As good: the sash cords run free again
And I am leaning out and calling them
To hurry now and join us quickly, will they,
Quickly – we are all ready to begin.

Flood

We live in the promise of miraculous lakes:
Dagenham, Greenwich, Wapping, the Isle of Dogs.

'When the siren sounds, those in the blue environs
Should proceed immediately to non-risk zones.'

Spring tides, high winds: for days we can hear
Of nothing else, our eyes bright with disaster,

Our dreams a chronicle of *mountaing anarchie*,
The river-folke frantick, shippës trappt in trees.

And the dove we sent out, when it came back,
Had the brown glaze of estuaries on its beak.

In our dreams no sandbags hold back the flood:
We would bring the whole world down if we could.

A Provincial Fiction

These fields are pale with the myth
of faithless sons gone south
to the 'airs and graces of the city'.

All's lost through the loss of them:
hands dwindle at the farm
and the woods are a sighing of chainsaws.

Doctor says there's little hope.
Will you be coming up?
We've kept your room just as it always was.

The stone fires, the piebald hide
of hillsides under broken cloud,
these grounds they had and will not go back on.

Metamorphoses of Childhood

1

With my pair of labradors I lay
Like Romulus under the kitchen table.

We'll be back at six, my parents would say,
Abandoning me to the wolf-toothed nanny.

High above me her hands were baking
On a floured, unreachable shelf.

Later came squabbles with my fat twin-sister:
I was the handier, it seemed,

And to prove it constructed in days
A bakelite replica of Burnley.

2

The train runs right through the middle of the house . . .
Well, almost: they were the giants in our hedge,

Breathing fire from their sooty toppers,
The burdens of the world on their back.

They were fetching for magnates:
Coal, cotton, shearings of quarry.

Cars queued up to hear them at the crossing.
Our teacups trembled on tenterhooks.

I pined for release from the attic room
Where a slip of the tongue had confined me.

3

Misery had no bedtime: it fell
Like lead in the middle of the night.

Boum, boum, boum, boum — it was the sound
Of boredom in my bloodstream,

The high room coming and going.
Why would the cornices never stay still?

First I was an elephant,
Then a pin in the infinite spaces.

Marapa, marapa, I'd cry,
But my parents never heard me.

4

Where there's muck, there's brass they said,
As in the coppery shine of cow-pats.

But then I discovered the salt-lick,
A sort of blue whetstone lighting up the fields.

I'd been reading Scott Fitzgerald's
'The Diamond as Big as the Ritz'

And carried it home like a pools-win,
A sapphire from the mud. When I learnt the truth

It shrank in my grasp like an ice-pack:
I wept to be a prisoner of fact.

5

Death sauntered in adjoining rooms,
Familiar and airy as linen.

It was the dent in granpa's chair,
His saying *night-night* and never returning.

Heaven must be nice: his coffin
Looked plusher than a chocolate box.

And hell was just a nettle-sting
Or scorch from fireworks – only ages to heal.

Why, then, Daddy's tear, lying like a lens
On my new pointy-black shoes?

Cuckoo-pint

A brown matchstick held up in the wind,
the bract-leaf cupped around it like a palm.

March had not extinguished it: there it smirked,
sly as something done behind the sheds,

slithering from its half-unrolled umbrella
as we snipped pussy-willow from the lanes.

To come instead on this old man of the woods,
tanned and cowled and clammed inside his collar,

his shirt-front splattered with tobacco stains,
his poker oozy with tuber-froth,

was like learning by accident a secret
intended for later, exciting

and obscene and not to be gone back on,
like the knowledge of atoms, or death.

Pomagne

'Be careful not to spill it when it pops.
He'd bloody crucify me if he caught us.'

We had taken months to get to this,
our first kiss a meeting of stalagmite

and stalactite. The slow drip of courtship:
her friend, June, interceding with letters,

the intimate struggle each Friday
under the Plaza's girder of light.

But here we were at last, drinking Pomagne
in her parents' double bed, Christmas Eve

and the last advent-calendar door.
'Did you hear the gate click?' 'No, did you?'

Mates

They are holed up in some bar among the dives
of Deptford, deep in their cups and a packet
of cashew nuts, like Chippy Hackee and cute
little Timmy Tiptoes hiding from their wives.

Any minute now they'll be talking shop
about some crony's record-breaking bender,
like that mate of Terry's banned from his own do
after sinking twenty vodkas and a cop.

Set them up again: I'm holding my tankard
so the cloudy light will set them up –
this mermaid on a forearm, that chinstrap
of a scar – though I'll try not to look hard

for fear of finding myself there, out on the piss
with a black-eyed, sulphurous misogynist.

Him

Like an Arctic fox snapping up grounded guillemot
   chicks
he hangs out in the parks and wastegrounds, the id of
   cities,
for time to bring her to this pretty pass.

Something has broken from the front of his mind
leaving just the back of it, a daubed cave of hunters and
   hunted
where no one but these girls can be allowed.

So he waits for them, leggy like deer in their ankle socks,
loud with an innocence he takes for the lack of it,
full of themselves, full of their mums and dads.

This one especially, wet-eyed as a leveret:
at the corners of sight she flickers like a red ignition light,
coming and going in her striped neck-scarf and PVC mac.

And soon there'll be a day she peels off from the others –
a buckle to be fastened, a brooch to be gone back for –
and then will be the time to introduce himself.

She is the special one who'll grow up in his care,
if she would only stop that screaming, if she could only
be made to understand him, but this is the only way.

Working in lines like beaters at a grouse-shoot,
we go on searching, stony among ferns and bracken,
unable to spring her from his trap.

The Ballad of the Yorkshire Ripper

The 'Red Death' had long devastated the country. No pestilence had ever been so fatal, or so hideous. Blood was its Avatar and its seal . . .

– Edgar Allan Poe, 'The Masque of the Red Death'

I were just cleaning up streets our kid. Just cleaning up streets.
– Peter Sutcliffe to his brother Carl, as quoted in Gordon Burn's
Somebody's Husband, Somebody's Son

Ower t'ills o Bingley
stormclouds clap an drain,
like opened blood-black blisters
leakin pus an pain.

Ail teems down like stair-rods,
an swells canals an becks,
an fills up studmarked goalmouths,
an bursts on mind like sex.

Cos sex is like a stormclap,
a swellin in thi cells,
when lightnin arrers through thi
an tha knows there in't owt else.

Ah've felt it in misen, like,
ikin ome part-fresh
ower limestone outcrops
like knuckles white through flesh:

ow men clap down on women
t'old em there for good
an soak up all their softness
an lounder em wi blood.

67

It's then I think on t'Ripper
an what e did an why,
an ow mi mates ate women,
an ow Pete med em die.

I love em for misen, like,
their skimmerin lips an eyes,
their ankles light as jinnyspins,
their seggy whisps an sighs,

their braided locks like catkins,
an t'curlies glashy black,
the peepin o their linnet tongues,
their way o cheekin back.

An ah look on em as kindred.
But mates all say they're not,
that men must have t'owerance
or world will go to rot.

Lad-loupin molls an gadabouts,
fellow-fond an sly,
flappy-skets an drabbletails
oo'll bleed a bloke bone-dry:

that's ow I ear em spoke of
when lads are on their tod,
an ow tha's got to leather em
to stop em gi'in t'nod.

An some o t'same in Bible
where Paul screams fit to bust
ow men are fallen creatures
but womenfolk are t'wust.

Now I reckon this fired Peter,
an men-talk were is goad,
an culprit were our belderin God
an is ancient, bullyin road.

No, Pete weren't drove by vengeance,
rountwistedness or ale,
but to show isen a baufy man –
but let me tell thi tale.

*

Peter worked in a graveyard,
diggin bone an sod.
From t'grave of a Pole, Zapolski,
e eard – e reckoned – God,

sayin: 'Lad, tha's on a mission,
ah've picked thi out o t'ruck.
Go an rip up prostitutes.
They're nobbut worms an muck.

'Streets are runnin sewers.
Streets are open sores.
Get in there wi thi scalpel
an wipe away all t'oors.'

Pete were pumped like a primus.
E felt is cravin whet.
E started cruisin Chapeltown
but e didn't kill, not yet.

E took a job on t'lorries,
a Transcontinental Ford.
E felt reet good in t'cabin.
E felt like a bloody Lord.

E'd bin a bit of a mardy,
angin on t'old dear's skirt.
E didn't like folks shoutin,
or scraps wi lads, or dirt.

E'd watch his dad trough offal –
trotters, liver, tripe –
or pigeon scraped from t'by-pass,
or rabbit, ung an ripe,

an all e'd felt were babbyish,
a fustilugs, alf-nowt,
an wished e were is younger kid
tekkin lasses out.

But now e'd started truckin
an ropin up is load
an bought isen a Bullworker
e swelled up like a toad,

an stuck is ead in motors
an messed wi carbs an ubs,
an drove wi mates to Manningham
an other arse-end pubs,

or sometimes off to Blackpool
to t'Tower or lights or pier,
or waxworks Chamber of Orrors –
aye, Pete were allus theer.

E met a lass called Sonia,
a nervy type, a shrew,
oo mithered im an nattered,
but Pete, e thought she'd do.

She seemed a cut above im,
a teacher, arty too,
oo wanted summat more'n kids.
Aye, Pete, e thought she'd do.

Cos Sonia, she weren't mucky,
not like yon other bags,
them tarts in fishnet stockins,
them goers, buers, slags.

*

Voice said 'Lad, get crackin:
ah've med thi bombardier.'
Pete blasted red-light districts,
eight lasses in two year.

E slit em up on waste-ground,
in ginnel, plot an park,
in cemetery an woodyard,
an allus after dark.

Is tools were ball-pein ammers,
acksaws an carvin knives,
an a rusty Phillips screwdriver
oned for endin lives.

Cops dint fuss wi fust three,
paid to out on street,
though e blunted blade on is Stanley
deguttin em like meat.

Nor minded marks on fourth lass,
ripped up in her flat,
wi both ends on a clawammer,
split-splat, split-splat, split-splat.

But Jayne MacDonald were a shopgirl
sellin nobbut shoes.
Pete, e killed er anyway
an now e were front page noos.

They appointed a Special Detective,
George Oldfield e were called.
E looked like a country bumpkin,
puffin, red, alf-bald.

E fixed up a Ripper Freefone,
Leeds 5050,
an asked Joe Soap to ring im up
an 'Tell us what you know.'

An folks, they give im names all right:
cousins, neighbours, mates,
blokes what they didn't tek to –
all were candidates.

But Pete, no e weren't rumbled.
E moved to a slap-up ouse,
pebbledash an wi a garden,
an utch to keep is mouse.

Cos Sonia, though she nittered
an med im giddyup,
were potterin too long in t'attic
to mind that owt were up.

An she went so ard at paintin
an scrubbin on ands an knee
she nivver noticed blood on trews
an t'missin cutlery.

*

Two weeks afore they'd folks roun
to drink to movin in
Pete ad topped another lass
an not a soul ad sin.

Now, after tekkin guests ome,
e went to t'mouldy corpse
an slashed it wi a glass pane
an serrated neck wi saws.

E were a one-man abattoir.
E cleavered girls in alves.
E shishkebab'd their pupils.
E bled em dry like calves.

Their napes as soft as foxglove,
the lovely finch-pink pout,
the feather-fern o t'eyelash –
e turned it all to nowt.

Seventh lass e totted
were in Garrads Timberyard.
E posted corpse in a pinestack
like Satan's visitin card.

Eighth were a badly woman
oo'd just come off o t'ward
o Manchester Royal Infirmary
an went back stiff as board.

E id is next on a wastetip
under a sofa's wings.
E stuffed her mouth wi ossair.
Er guts poked through like springs.

An wee Jo Whitaker, just 19,
an Alifax Buildin clerk,
bled from er smashed-egg foread
till t'gutter ran sump-dark.

There were lorry-oil inside er,
an filins in each pore,
which might ave led to Peter
if police ad looked some more.

But Oldfield, e weren't tryin.
E'd ears for nobbut 'Jack':
some oaxer wi a cassette tape
ad sent im reet off track.

Voice on tape were a Geordie's,
a tauntin, growlin loon:
'They nivver learn, George, do they.
Nice chattin. See you soon.'

George fell line an sinker,
a fishook in is pride:
'E thinks e's cock o t'midden
but I'll see that Jack inside.'

Aye, George e took it personal,
a stand-up, man to man,
like a pair o stags wi orns locked
– but Ripper offed an ran,

an wi George left fightin boggarts
e struck again like bleach:
bang in t'middle o Bradford
e wiped out Barbara Leach.

Then Marguerite Walls in Farsley,
strangled wi a noose
(a change from t'usual colander job,
none o t'normal clues).

*

Everyweer in Yorkshire
were a creepin fear an thrill.
At Elland Road fans chanted
'Ripper 12 Police Nil.'

Lasses took up karate,
judo an self-defence,
an jeered at lads in porn shops,
an scrawled stuff in pub Gents,

like: 'Ripper's not a psychopath
but every man in pants.
All you blokes would kill like him
given half a chance.

'Listen to your beer-talk –
"hammer", "poke" and "screw",
"bang" and "score" and "lay" us:
that's what the Ripper does too.'

Aye, e did it again one last time,
to a student, Jacqueline Hill,
in a busy road, wi streetlights,
in a way more twisted still,

blammin er wi is Phillips –
but rest o that ah'll leave,
out o respect to t'family
an cos it meks me eave.

Now cops stepped up on pressure.
George, e got is cards.
Files were took from is ands
an put in Scotland Yard's.

They talked to blokes on lorries
an called at Pete's ouse twice,
but Sonia allus elped im out
wi rock-ard alibis.

It were fluke what finally nabbed im.
E'd parked is car in t'gates
of a private drive in Sheffield
wi ripped-off numberplates.

Lass oo e'd got wi im
were known to work this patch.
Cops took em both to t'station
but adn't twigged yet, natch.

Ad e meant to kill er?
E'd brought an ammer an knife
but maundered on alf evenin
ow e cunt stand sight o t'wife.

Then lass passed im a rubber
an come on all coquettish.
But still e didn't touch er.
It were like a sort o death-wish.

E managed to ide is tackle
sayin e wanted a pee.
But later on is ammer
were found by a young PC.

So cops they lobbed im questions
through breakfast, dinner, tea,
till e said: 'All right, you've cracked it.
Ripper, aye, it's me.

'Ah did them thirteen killins.
Them girls live in mi brain,
mindin me o mi evil.
But ah'd do it all again.

'Streets are runnin sewers.
Streets are open sores.
Ah went there wi mi armoury
to wipe away all t'oors.

'Ah were carrying out God's mission.
Ah were followin is commands.
E pumped me like a primus.
Ah were putty in is ands.'

                    *

This were nub o t'court case:
were Peter reet or mad?
If lawyer could prove im a nutter
e'd not come off as bad.

Were e bats as a bizzum
or t'devil come from ell?
Choice were life in a mental
or a Parkhurst prison cell.

E sat in dock like a gipsy
wi is open sky-blue shirt
an gawped at judge an jury
as if all t'lot were dirt.

Defence called up their experts,
psychiatrists an such,
oo sed Pete weren't no sadist
an didn't rate sex much,

that e'd suffered paranoia,
allucinations too,
an killed cos is mind ad drove im —
so t'gravestone tale were true.

But t'other lot med mincemeat
o those who'd bin Pete's dupe
showin ow e'd outflanked em
to get isen from t'soup.

Cos why, if e were loopy,
ad e allus killed on t'dot,
Friday nights an Saturdays,
in cold blood not in ot?

An why, if e weren't no sadist,
ad e left girls, more 'n once,
wi a hundred stabs in t'breastbone
an planks shoved up their cunts?

An ad he shown repentance
for 't'lasses' or for 't'oors'?
As for t'religious mission:
e'd med it up, of course.

(All through this Pete's bearin
were cold as marble slab,
ard as a joint from t'freezer,
slant as a Scarborough crab.)

Counsels rested cases.
Jury reasoned it through.
Judge said: 'How do you find him?'
'Guilty – ten to two.'

They oiked im off in a wagon
past lynchers urlin abuse
an placards urgin t'government
BRING BACK CAT AND NOOSE.

They took im to Parkhurst Prison
to serve is time an more,
an folks said t'other inmates
would know to settle t'score.

But when is face were taloned
wi a broken coffee jar
it weren't for rippin real flesh
but nudes from t'prison *Star*.

An meanwhile rest o t'Sutcliffes
spent up their Fleet Street brass,
an put the boot in Sonia:
'Job's all down to t'lass.

'Our Pete were nivver a nutter.
E'd allus a smile on t'face.
That Sonia nagged im rotten
till e killed oors in er place.

'Cos that's the rub wi women,
they push us blokes too far
till us can't be eld responsible
for bein what us are.'

*

So tha sees, nowt's really altered
though Peter's out o t'way.
Mi mates still booze an charnel.
Weather's same each day.

Ower t'ills up northways
stormclouds thump an drain
like opened blood-black blisters
leakin pus an pain.

An death is like a stormclap,
a frizzlin o thi cells,
a pitchfork through thi arteries,
an tha knows there in't owt else.

It meks me think on Peter,
an what e did an why,
an ow mi mates ate women,
an ow Pete med em die.

Ah love em for misen, like,
their skimmerin lips an eyes,
their ankles light as jinnyspins,
their seggy whisps an sighs,

tiny tarn o t'navel,
chinabowl o t'ead,
steppin cairns o t'backbone,
an all e left for dead.

An ah look on em as kindred.
But mates all say they're not,
that men must ave t'owerance
or world will go to rot.

An Pete were nobbut a laikin
o this belderin, umped-up God,
an served is words an logic
to rivet girls to t'sod.

An I don't walk appily out no more
now lasses fear lad's tread,
an mi mates call me a Bessy,
an ah dream of all Pete's dead,

an ow they come again to me,
an we croodle out o eye
in nests o fern an floss-seave
an fillytails in t'sky,

an ah mend em all wi kindness
as we kittle out on t'fells
an learn us t'ease o human love
until there in't owt else.

Fuel Debts Inquiry

When I surveyed the wondrous New Cross blocks,
layers of eyes froze behind spyholes.

'I can/cannot afford to heat my living-room':
interviewers circle as appropriate.

The flats massed like an iceberg, nine-tenths in the blue,
strung together by a lift I did not dare take.

Rung after rung I mounted, rang down corridors,
hung about for answers twenty floors up.

Inscrutable, screwed to the wood, threshold lenses
telescoped my well-meant profile.

Dogs barked, carpeted steps secretly came and went,
the Cyclops stare guarded all who dwelt in there.

I did/did not establish who was in arrears.
I could get some/no statistics on the coldness inside.

We Won't Get Fooled Again

Among the Saturday bargains – hose pipes,
open-crotch panties, inflatable chairs –
this one: 'Front-door spyhole. Six-foot span.
You see unwanted callers. They don't see you.'

The picture's inspired. A curlered housewife
safe behind her door figures immediately
the scar-faced stranger looming outside
is not selling brushes. She won't open up.

Europe's new frontier! The end of the terror!
Never again those games of happy families
cut short by a rap in the heart of the door –
father leaving us to answer it,
then the loud, unfamiliar voices
and the silence for a moment or two.

Theory of Heredity

The generations come down on you –
like football crowds when a goal is scored.

It began when a sperm, waving its scarf excitedly,
tick-ticked its way in through the turnstile.

Now it's reached hundreds – parents, and their parents,
and the ones before that, stacked on the terraces

as high as sight, and you're at the bottom.
And when their tassels heave like a harvest-field

you will heave along, though you thought
by now you could go which way you pleased.

The Editor Regrets

Had they poisoned the envelopes? For seven years
I had to vet Imagination,
the dribs and drabs of metrical invention,
and send the rejects back in sae's.

My in-tray filled with memos from the psyche,
this man's ecstasy and that one's pain,
how stallion's dung resembles a cairn,
or what we are to think of Nagasaki.

And most of it no good, so that I knew
one day I would die quite horribly
licking the seal of a fanatic, my
antagonist, my brother in failure, you.

'What trust would be like they never . . .'
Nope. But I let my guard dog lick the envelope.

Pendle Witches

On recs and at swimming pools
we searched for the girl
– shy and uncomeatable –
through whose glimming thigh-tops

the light would make a perfect O,
that florin emptiness
not the token of a virgin
but the hole in a lemmel-stone

to ward off the hags
who ran the Pennines
and who wanted to trap us
in the sossy peat of their maw.

Epithalamion

Cart-tracks, drove-roads,
coast-paths and bridle-ways,
lanes banked high with campion and rose:

along the dotted lines of England
we signed away one summer
mile after mile after mile.

A Child in Winter

Where is the man who does not feel his heart softened . . . [by] these
so helpless and so perfectly innocent little creatures?

— Cobbett

When the trees have given up,
snowberries come into their own,
winter grapes, albino
settlers of the dark.

With their milky blobs
they lined our doorstep
that November dusk
we swung your basket

up the gravel-path
and home. Child-Moses,
prince of the changing-mat,
heir of furry ducklings,

your babygros in drifts
on the clothes-rack,
we anoint your body's
rashes and folds.

When you cry it's like
some part of ourselves
breaking off and filling
these rooms with its pain.

Your breath's a matchflame
certain to go out,
we're at the cot hourly
holding our own.

In the shush of night-time
snowflakes crowd the window
like our own pale faces,
a shedding of old skins,

a blown seedhead,
paper pellets thrown down
by the gods to mark
your fiftieth day.

Lorries flounder on the hill.
We're out there watching
with a babysling
while the world goes under wool.

Little one, limpet,
resented stranger,
who has no time for me
and does not know time,

your home's the cradle
of a snowy hillfort
with pink turrets
and underground springs.

Daylight bores you: all night
you otter in our bed until
we wake to find you with us,
hands folded like a saint

accepting his death.
If it's we who must die first
that seems less costly now,
having you here like wheat.

Spring comes, measured
in light and celandines
and your first tooth, faint
as a rock at low tide,

headstone for these trials
with cottonbuds and nappies,
your silver lips tracking
for comfort in the dark.

Sleep On It

Wrecked by our children
we sit among the spars
of a Chinese take-away,
washed up and hollow-eyed,
hanging on for nothing
but the Epilogue,
two ruined late-late lives.

Another night ahead
of waking from sleep's seabed
to the cry of a kittiwake,
a *waaa-waaa* dragging me
blind towards the child
among wave-tossed bedsheets
howling to be airlifted free.

The compulsion of people
to remake themselves
could die in a room like this,
a graveyard of ambition
where hopes lie scattered
with the lego, a city
just abandoned or sacked . . .

But we'll be right again
by morning as light or love
haloes every game they play –
Seth grounded with his balsa
plane, Aphra all at sea
in her own puddle which glimmers
like a dropped silk dress.

Meningococcus

'My son has gone under the hill.
We called him after a clockmaker
but God meets all such whimsy
with his early-striking hands.

That night of his high fever
I held a stream against me,
his heart panicky as a netted bird,
globes of solder on his brow.

Then he was lost in sea-fret,
the other side of silence,
his eyes milky as snowberries
and his fifteen months unlearned.

They have taken him away
who was just coming to me,
his spine like the curve
of an avocet's bill.'

Somebody Loves Us All

I was tired, I suppose, and then hit ice,
no means of steering with the steering wheel,
the car sheering off into the crash rail,
the children waking with synchronized cries –

which is why we are here, in the lit hen-hut
of Motorway Recoveries, Snodland,
where an ESSO-hearted garage-hand
presses through the carbon of our invoice, not

rude exactly but unable to share
the drama of this happening to us,
the wall behind him trophied with photos
of his breakdown truck posed by the remainder

of Maestros and Escorts from which no one
could have passed on to this breathing-space
or heard their name read out into the mouthpiece
of a fingermarked, oil-anointed phone.

Superstore

Sunday, late, at the superstore,
a fresh wind across the car park
plaining through the trolley's mesh,
and doors that slide apart
on a carnival of promo flags,
a vault of infinite shelves.

Baths, tiles, kiddyseats, barbecues,
woodfiller, Polyfilla, turps,
clocks and radios
separate or in wedlock,
pinewood pews set under smoky tabletops,
rolls of insulation that brings us

round a corner to PRODUCE —
coley and fish fingers,
French loaves and granary loaves,
apples and potatoes laid out
as for Harvest festival
beside a fan of dried-up flowers.

I could go on, and do go on,
past the fly-mos on a prickly strip
of astroturf, the wheel-less wheelbarrows,
the grass seed, weedkiller, lawn feed,
the gnomes fishing lucklessly
in the pre-mould of a pond.

And beyond to the fashion grove,
the aisles of dresses waiting there
like princesses for the awakening touch,
the coat-hangers like Cupid's bows
carried off to screened confessionals
and mirrored revisions of old selves.

But that's enough for now: we heave
the trolley to the log-jammed checkout
where girls with singing typewriters
record our losses onto spools
of print-out which they hand us
with an absent smile.

Then out onto the tarmac
past a car boot spilling over
with the corpses of cement bags
and a man and his wife shouting
at each other like Pyramus and Thisbe
through the vents in a louvre door.

And there's not much left of Sunday,
dusk lowering on the roof-racks,
another weekend gone into nothing
as the red-eyed tail-lights
file through the barriered tollgate,
leaving behind the superstore,

its row of lights like the buttons
on a keyboard, its glowing crypts
not a mockery of churches
but a way like them of forgetting
the darkness where no one's serving
and there's nothing to choose from at all.

Our Domestic Graces

The Chancellor of Gifts is an elitist.
You can't pretend he'll step out of the night
With a gilt invitation-card or flowers.
The brilliant words we wrote down in a dream
Aren't there beside our bedside after all.

Yet something calls from the great expanse
Of air we have made our latest home in.
Studio voices wake us near eight
With stories of God and how 'He moves among us
Constantly like light'. What are his tracks like?

Mystery starts no further away
Than these mossy footprints crossing the lawn
To where the raspberries are ripe again
And the panes of the greenhouse brim with tears.
Today even our lost city appears

From its shroud: a white dust-sheet slowly lifts
And here are all our glinting heirlooms –
The gasworks, like a coronet, queens it
Over the houses, and bridges grace
The river with their lacy hems and Vs.

To have it all so clear – the congregating
Chimneypots, the lines of traffic passing
Over the heath like words being typed on a page.
Christ's fishermen must have felt like this,
Crying out, amazed, at their spangled catch.

Light falls about these rooms, silvering the face
Of what we are most used to, and ourselves,
Who on such days might think we had been
Elected at last – guest musicians
At the garden party of the gods.

A Concise Definition of Answers

The city calls with its arches and spires
While the flatlands flourish with incest.
There are more curious things I wanted,
If possible, to touch on today –
How the sky, for instance, on these sultry afternoons
Seems to settle round your forehead,

Or the link between nostalgia and smell.
At this point science comes in, as you might expect,
Or as you might yourself come in with that
Colander of raspberries and rain. It seems like
Everything we hoped for, as if the mayor had cut the tape
And events might finally begin.

But look, there's a storm blowing up, the sky
Flickering like an old TV and the volume
Almost deafening. Answers: I was holding them here
Just now but they are gone again into those
Cloud-lit days where martins and swifts sweep low
Over the ground but can turn up nothing.

Dark Glasses

And take upon 's the mystery of things
As if we were God's spies . . .
              – *King Lear*

The privacies of lace and leylandii,
The pseudonym to climb through like a trap-door.
The dark falling as you enter what was said
In the summer-house, behind the Chubb,
Beyond the entryphone, inside the glass-topped wall.
What nestled through customs in a hub-cap.
What you must never mention to anyone.
For God's sake, Harry Lime, hold your tongue.

Or this other sort, let's-be-candid-please,
Big Mouth, the soul of indiscretion,
The gust that took the trellis clean away.
This Norfolk skyline, vast and open-hearted,
Levels with its questioners, or seems to,
For though we left with a full confession
By the time we played the tape back that evening
It had reverted to a row of noughts.

Either way you come out none the wiser.
She is silky and elusive, returns
At twelve dripping beads from a broken necklace,
An accident, a little job for you
(A job to ignore the flush in her cheekbones
And the departure of a misted car).
And this – how you love it – is mystery,
Wrapping itself around you like a bride.

But something cries out to be resolved.
The pen moves off with its search parties.
There are footlights on the dipped horizon,
As if the ones whose plot we are part of
Were on the brim of coming clear. It's late
But they'll be here by nightfall, you know they will.
Just as you despair their red torches
Flash through the dark like fluke late raspberries.

Kit Wright

Tune for an Ice Cream Van

And after many days he came
To seek his love in Kensington

Whom he had wronged in Hanger Lane
And lost in Kew. Then all around

The Brompton Cemetery the trees
Shook candid blossom in his eyes

That sought her everywhere. The ground
Betrayed no footprint. She achieved

No mention on the wind that splayed
His hunger down the Goldhawk Road

Past Hammersmith. Yet this thing stayed:
Her absence, in a glove-shaped cloud

Trailing the river, curling back
Past Fulham Broadway. Round he went

Till there at Parsons Green he slowed
His steps, and sat, and cried aloud:

'Down all the skies and miles of eyes
There's no one knows her now!' The day

Darkened him into Chelsea. When
He crossed the river it was night.

Upon his journey two stars leant.
Which her, no knowing. Still he sent

Steps echoing through Clapham, gone
Too far between two stars to know

He travelled by his own sad light
And there was nowhere else to go.

At last, his strength and spirit done,
He whispered to his sons her name

And how it was, and how he came
To seek his love in Kensington,

Her whom he wronged in Hanger Lane
And lost in Kew. Aggrieved he lies

And still it falls, and still they come,
The desperate blossom in their eyes.

The Captain

I liked the Captain, all the seams
He fell apart at, going mad

Because he thought the shivered elms
Would fall upon his ashen head

And swifts would peck his eyes. Bad dreams
Can't take the quickness that he had

Who flighted slow leg-breaks that swung
In from the off, then looped away,

Or, lolled on August vapours, hung
And came through flat and how was that?

I liked the Captain, all his schemes
For harassing the right hand bat.

I liked the Captain, all his themes
And each strange learned word he said

Who read solely Victoriana
And had by heart half *Silas Marner*

Along with odd tunes in his head:
He thought the swifts would peck his eyes.

They shall not cut him down to size
Nor seek to break his flighted mind

In institutions. Nothing dead
But he shall be restored again.

Elms shall respect unshaven brain
And birds his wisdom. World needs him.

Come all, come any revolution,
The Captain is the man for spin.

January Birth

For Caroline Maclean

Brightest splinter, scarlet berry,
   On the shivered world you lay,
Sliver from the tree of winter
   When the hawthorn held no may,
When the London plane was childless
   And the dark was in the day.

From her labour then your mother
   Freely wept to see you wake,
Take this crying star for neighbour:
   Wept with joy for your fierce sake,
Heart of light in snowing darkness,
   Storm of love and glistening flake.

O tender head, bare tree that branches
   Veins in perilous array,
May the violent day defend you.
   Want for nothing, little clay.
O cup of air, O moth-light wingbeat,
   Darling, bear the world away.

A New World Symphony

What plucky sperm invented Mrs Gale?
(All starless in her first degree lay she.)

What head-of-the-river victor
plunged for her sake
down to the makings of a whale
in the amniotic sea?

Fortune the germ.
(Luck likewise it took
to get to be a sperm.)

Oh
the little bit kept its head and it flashed its tail
and there on the leaking waters –
furious, mauve, harpooned to life –
was Mrs Gale, I'm glad to say,
a beautiful daughter to Mr and Mrs Elkins,
to Mr Gale: a bouncing wife.

Time out of mind so many minds
prized out of time to consider the light of day!
Let us rejoice in the work of the sperm
and that of the fortunate egg in Mrs Elkins
(the role of its life to play)
who made Mrs Gale for our delight
as, happily, we
freely may.

Packer's Circuit

Something about this game
eternally fades, to bring
the lost outfielders in,

those whited ruminants
under the layers of green
whom old men at the field-edge

dream, dead name by name,
that played the day with a weeping
willow for ashes, ashes,

till you could believe, by a thin
tide of shadow that washes
play to its close, the ball

swung most sharply in tear-gas,
the rotten grave took spin,
a ghost could make a hundred

with the board of a coffin lid
and Father Time himself
scythe off his balls and sing

for something about this game
eternally fades, to bring
the lost outfielders in.

Red Boots On

Way down Geneva,
All along Vine,
Deeper than the snow drift
Love's eyes shine:

Mary Lou's walking
In the winter time.

She's got

Red boots on, she's got
Red boots on,
Kicking up the winter
Till the winter's gone.

So

Go by Ontario,
Look down Main,
If you can't find Mary Lou,
Come back again:

Sweet light burning
In winter's flame.

She's got

Snow in her eyes, got
A tingle in her toes
And new red boots on
Wherever she goes

So

All around Lake Street,
Up by St Paul,
Quicker than the white wind
Love takes all:

Mary Lou's walking
In the big snow fall.

She's got

Red boots on, she's got
Red boots on,
Kicking up the winter
Till the winter's gone.

A Doll's House

A man sat staring at a doll's house
Hour after hour and more and more
He believed. He could see
In the kitchenette two personettes
And one of them was standing in the sink
And one lay on the floor.

The man stared more and more.

The bed in the bathroom was neatly made up with a
Pink eiderdown neatly made up from a
Pink ribbon. But no one was in the bed
And no one was in the bathroom.
Only a horse
Was trying the door.

The man stared more and more.

Then softly the man went in,
Edged down
Past the creaky banisters, down
He crept
To the hall, hid nimbly
Behind a cow.

From the sink: 'My dear,
That tractor's on the roof again, I fear.'
Sadly from the floor: 'These nights
It seems to be always there.'

Then silence between
Personette A and Personette B,
Now like a matchstick drumming a plastic thimble,
Now like the sea.

From the sink: 'How I wish, my dear,
That you and I could move house.
But these matters are not in our hands. Our directives
Come from above.'
Said the floor: 'How can we ever move house
When the house keeps moving, my love?'

A man sat staring at a doll's house
Hour after hour and more and more
He believed he could see
Perspectives of the terrorized world,
Delicate, as a new-tooled body,
Monstrous, mad as he.

The Council of the Gods

Lay no blame. Have pity.
Put your fingers in the wounds of the committee.

They never reached your item.
Disputing Item One *ad infinitum*.

Lay no blame. Be tender.
The retrospective start of the agenda

Was all they managed treating.
Consider, pray, the feeling of the meeting.

(They felt awful.) Not surprising
They never came to matters not arising

From Matters Arising:

> *Who took the chair when the standing committee last sat?*
> *Who kept the minutes for hours and hours and hours?*
> *Who tabled the motion,*
> *Who motioned the table*
> *Whereat*
> *The standing committee*
> *Sat?*

Have pity.
Put your fingers in the wounds of the committee.

The gods have not been sleeping.
All night they sat, in grief and boredom, weeping.

The Adventures of Patience

Patience was God's smallest moon.
She waited in the wings.

No, said Daddy,
No, said Daddy,
Not without a safety net:
Not yet.

Nightly in turn her voluptuous sisters, Gloria and Diana,
Bicycled on a tightrope over the mountains,
Surfed on the spray of the clouds,
Skimmed like Frisbees over the wailing waters
And Patience waited.

Daddy, she said, there is so little time
For my little turn.
I need to dispense an inquisitive healing light
On broken things. I do know how –
Daddy,
Am I on now?

Too soon,
Too soon,
My little moon.

And so she waited.
Below her the great green platitude
Hustled and boomed, thudded and shuffled forever,
Land clanged open, roared and reset,
In and out of each other's delicate bones
The creatures flickered, the bombs flowered,
The earth buried
And the earth bore.

Daddy, said Patience, what am I waiting *for*?

Wait a bit more, said Daddy,
Wait just a bit more.

Till the land was a hole she waited,
Till the sea drained from its trough.
Right, said Daddy, go!

And Patience said, Daddy –

piss *off*?

Elizabeth

In the summer of 1968 thousands of people turned out at the small stations along the route to see the train carrying the body of Robert Kennedy from New York to Arlington National Cemetery in Washington. In Elizabeth, New Jersey, three people were pressed forward on to the line by the crowd and killed by a train coming the other way – I happened to be travelling up by the next train in this direction and passed the bodies. One was of a black woman.

Up from Philadelphia,
Kennedy on my mind,
Found you waiting in Elizabeth,
Lying there by the line.

Up from Philadelphia,
Wasn't going back,
Saw you, then saw your handbag
Forty yards on up the track.

Saw you under a blanket,
Black legs sticking through,
Thought a lot about Kennedy,
Thought a lot about you,

Years later,

Blood on the line, blood on the line,
Elizabeth,
No end, no end to anything,
Nor any end to death.

No public grief by television,
Weeping all over town,
Nobody locked the train up
That struck the mourners down.

Nobody came to see you,
You weren't lying in state.
They swept you into a siding
And said the trains would be late.

They left you there in the siding
Against an outhouse wall
And the democratic primaries,
Oh they weren't affected at all,

In no way,

Blood on the line, blood on the line,
Elizabeth,
No end, no end to anything,
Nor any end to death.

Sirhan shot down Kennedy,
A bullet in L.A.,
But the one that broke Elizabeth,
It was coming the other way,

Coming on out of nowhere,
Into nowhere sped,
Blind as time, my darling,
Blind nothing in its head.

Elizabeth, Oh Elizabeth,
I cry your name and place
But you can't see under a blanket,
You can't see anyone's face,

Crying

Blood on the line, blood on the line,
Elizabeth,
No end, no end to anything,
Nor any end to death.

Deathbed Observation

Broken in my father's face,
The lock of anguish and dismay,
   And lines of laughter – burned away
   In death that turned his body grey.

Fell no dark upon that place.
Death relit a younger grace.
   Strange, in his own light, he lay
   And he was handsome as the day.

Here Come Two Very Old Men

Here come two very old men of exquisite caution
Who handle each other like costly pieces of china
In the perilous matter of sitting down at the bar,

And you'd think it the most demanding of all operations
Ever conducted by bodies that have come this far,
That so long ago came yelling from the vagina,

That woke the world to be sitting where they are.

Black Box

The star is falling so it prove a stone.
Flight Zero, moon, is flashing us goodbye.

Because we could not bear to be alone
We talked our deaths down nightly from the sky.

In darkness, in the Dreamtime, we have flown
Over the mountain where our picked bones lie.

Frankie and Johnny in 1955

Many of the men wore damned great flannel trousers
With double-breasted blazers. Double-breasted women wore
   blouses

With pleated skirts or shiny black haunch-hugging dresses
On the night and the morning of the twin unpleasantnesses –

His shooting, her hanging – while I myself wore shorts,
Snakebelt and aertex, suitable for summer sports,

When Albert Pierrepoint hanged Ruth Ellis high
In Holloway Prison and I was too young to cry –

She, to die. Poor Ruth, I say:
She whipped out a .38, blew her lover away.

Now, Ruth was the last woman hanged on British earth
And David Blakely was of moneyed birth –

Public school, army, obsessed with racing cars,
Which he talked about all the time in clubs and bars –

Was a total shit, some say, which I think untrue –
I think he was as much of a shit as me or you –

Some say he was charming and friendly – alas for charm –
The grave leaves never a trace – well, he did her harm,

But not as much harm as she did him that day
She whipped out a damned great gun and she blew him away.

Well, Ruth was the Little Club night-club manageress
And had been through, seen through, much distress

Long before the killing. She'd a war-time child
By a GI who ditched her, divorce suit filed

From a mad alcoholic dentist who smashed her about:
Then: semi-pro loving in clubs. No doubt

Of the matter at all, time worked her so
Little Ruth was as hard as nails and as soft as snow

And the hurt she felt, and the love, and the hate
She fired point-blank from a damned great .38.

Oh, the reason little Ruth was standing in the dock
Was she loved him in the morning and she loved him round the
  clock

But people were stealing him. Ruth said, 'Well,
Can't see my loving man here, I'll see him in hell' –

And she wanted to die, did die, which she needn't have done
But she said in court, with that Smith and Wesson gun

She'd a fancy to kill him – wed him with a big black trousseau?
Yes, she wanted to die. But *he* didn't wish to do so

And I count it a shame that by South End Green
She wasted her lover with a damned great hand-machine.

She'd a powder compact that played *La Vie En Rose*,
She was taking French lessons, she'd a special film-actress pose

For photos, she was slender, she'd a small white face like an ox-eyed
Daisy and hair of pure peroxide

(That probably hanged her – at the trial a smart
Juror noted down: 'She's a TYPICAL WEST END TART')

And Blakely was a handsome and a likeable youth –
Spoilt ponce, too, violent bastard to Ruth,

Some say. Who's to judge? Oh, the judge could judge that day
He slipped on his little black cap and he slid her away.

Not much to say. She loved him but she hadn't got him,
Waited by the pub and when he came out she shot him

With a mixed spray of bullets to his head, his lungs, his heart:
It was theatre, my lovely, performance art,

But you didn't want to do it, they didn't want to do it to you
And they snipped your pretty white throat pretty nearly in two

Because, entirely, it was 1955:
Oh, I wish you were here, I wish you were alive

And I wish above all things unmade, junked down the spout,
That damned great side-arm that took your loving man out.

Your lifetime later, I think how nothing is freed
By time from its shadow, opacity of need,

The instant when it happens, *in situ*, on spec –
How nothing but detail breaks anyone's heart or neck –

Of how, little Ruth, in the first year of rock-and-roll,
You could tip young David down into the hole

Or how they could hang you on a Holloway hanging tree,
Poor little Ruth Ellis, two months before ITV.

Hardly Believable Horace and Hattie in Hell

Horace and Hattie, in cacophonous concert,
  Lived to a dual and discordant tune,
They could and they did disagree about everything
  Under the sun, and also the moon,
And if one said, 'Nice morning', the other infallibly
  Pronounced it a horrible afternoon,
And if either one triumphed in a point at issue
  (And no point was not) then the victory balloon
Would be savagely pierced when the narrowest opening
  For vengeance was glimpsed. They did not commune:
They spoke to each other to accuse, to exclude,
  To ensnare and enrage, to impair and impugn.

Which makes it the stranger that they slept together
  Where even in the night like poisonous rain
Exchanged unpleasantries dripped in the darkness –
  Miss no chance where a particle of pain
Might yet be extracted was their changeless motto
  And no opportunity passed in vain –
So they sharpened themselves like knives on each other
  Where once more sweetly they had lain
When theirs was a house where love was living
  Whose ghost would not sleepwalk again,
Never a shadow, never a whisper,
  Not a whisker, not a grain.

So Hattie died, and she died with a rattle
  That threw the points in Horace's head
And his heart on its journey grated, slowed
  And turned like an engine in a turning-shed

And headed back down through the wailing tunnel
   Of the years, of the cold things done and said,
And he went by the land and he came by the water
   Of unshed tears on wounds unbled,
And he lay on his back in his clothes in the morning
   On that reconsecrated bed,
Floor of the ocean of a marriage, and cried
   Like the sea, 'My love, my love is dead!'

The Boys Bump-starting the Hearse

The hearse has stalled in the lane overlooking the river
Where willows are plunging their heads in the bottle-green
   water
        And bills of green baize drakes kazoo.
        The hearse has stalled and what shall we do?

The old don comes on, a string bag his strongbox.
He knows what is known about Horace but carries no tool box.
        Small boys shout in the Cambridge sun.
        The hearse has stalled and what's to be done?

Lime flowers drift in the lane to the baskets of bicycles,
Sticker the wall with yellow and powdery particles.
        Monosyllabic, the driver's curse.
        Everything fires. Except the hearse

Whose gastric and gastric whinnies shoot neutered tom cats
In through the kitchen flaps of back gardens where tomtits
        Wizen away from the dangling crust.
        Who shall restart the returned-to-dust?

Shrill and sudden as birds the boys have planted
Their excellent little shoulders against the lamented
        Who bumps in second. A fart of exhaust.
        On goes the don and the holocaust.

Dungoblin

Come down, come down, you long-serving ladies of
   pleasure,
To Hove, to Rottingdean,
Where sea, where privet hedge are green
And a Tory sky
Has the rebel geranium's measure:
To Southport or
Liskeard,

After so many years hard
At the coal face of the libido,
Mes poules pas de luxe, come down, come, *tirez-*
Vous doucement les rideaux
On peaceful evenings with pollarded poodles
(Forsaken the stand-up and cash-down canoodles),
Chihuahua and chocs and the box and the balm

Of Dungoblin.

Forgotten, the day job, the night job, the so-much-a-go
   job,
Abandoned, the blow job,
Come down,
O come away from Humping Town
And snooze where the little waves lick themselves like cats
Under the green head
And the old folks' flats

At Dungoblin.

From Cheshire

For Anna

Come home safe: I think of you driving
   Over the Runcorn Bridge in our senile car,
Its toothless ratchets, arthritic pistons conniving
   To take me away from wherever you are.

Its steering like that old prostitute working a living
   On Huskisson Street outside our door:
Its raggedy brake shoes thin as the wind, giving
   Nothing but ice to your foot on the floor.

Please come home: I think of you leaving
   For ever, coming from Cheshire, only the snow
And the night and the endless black road, no retrieving
   Of you: without me, wherever I go.

I Found South African Breweries Most Hospitable

Meat smell of blood in locked rooms I cannot smell it,
Screams of the brave in torture loges I never heard nor
   heard of
Apartheid I wouldn't know how to spell it,
None of these things am I paid to believe a word of
For I am a stranger to cant and contumely.
I am a professional cricketer.
My only consideration is my family.

I get my head down nothing to me or mine
Blood is geysering now from ear, from mouth, from eye,
How they take a fresh guard after breaking the spine,
I must play wherever I like or die
So spare me your news your views spare me your homily.
I am a professional cricketer.
My only consideration is my family.

Electrodes wired to their brains they should have had
   helmets,
Balls wired up they should have been wearing a box,
The danger was the game would turn into a stalemate,
Skin of their feet burnt off I like thick woollen socks
With buckskin boots that accommodate them roomily
For I am a professional cricketer.
My only consideration is my family.

They keep falling out of the window they must be clumsy
And unprofessional not that anyone told me,
Spare me your wittering spare me your whimsy,
Sixty thousand pounds is what they sold me
And I have no brain. I am an anomaly.
I am a professional cricketer.
My only consideration is my family.

The Power of Prayer

Very, very little of his garden
    Did God elect to seed.
The rest he leased to utter, outer blankness,
    Invaded by the rankness
        Of not a single weed.

Many, many mansions has his dwelling.
    His own bedsit is small.
A vast and speechless city crumbles round it.
    Never a one has found it
        Anywhere at all.

The Day Room

From Kendal Ward, Rainhill Mental Hospital

1

Many are non-plussed
By the unexpected behaviour of their clothes
And have mislaid forever
The art of wearing the face.

Gums wedged tight or mouths
Locked open in a scream that travels inward
Homelessly:

Here we all are on your holy mountain.

It's a little bit nippy up here on the mountain
For some are shivering, never
Stop shivering, also

Unseasonably warm. That man
Is caked with lava, head to hip.

2

Come in, come in,
Don't shut the door.
Take care your feet
Don't touch the floor.

Come on, come on.
Avoid the wall.
Whatever you do
Don't breathe at all.

Stand back, stand back.
What is it? Ask
But whisper through
Your cotton mask.

Back out. Make sure
The door is closed.
Now wash your hands
And burn your clothes.

3

Joan's mouth is a crematorium.
Six years after her husband died
It burns and bleeds and weeps, she cannot beat
His flaring ashes down with her tongue.

All in the mind, and pain
(What was said? What left unsaid?)
A child of the mind
That eats the mother.

The widow is burned alive.

4

Where cigarettes are the entire economy
Domestic policy is locker-love.
Pink stones to arm the military,
White coats for the judiciary,
One hall in hell for all of the above.

5

The male nurses, without exception,
Corpulent, good-natured,
Mustachioed forty-year-olds.
Five of them. How can this be?

They must have a club where they stand and swap
Rounds and jokes and mistakes and moustaches,
Taking each other's paunches
Like a pulse.

6

Our road's a green carbolic corridor
Off which on certain days the sun
Ripens in small groves. In one

I found her crying because she had lost her lipstick
And, so she said, her bones.

The sun poured down.

We found the lipstick, couldn't find the bones.

7

Unspeakable blue
Observed
Through unbreakable glass.

How long have those humanoid beech-limbs,
Their green-dust glaze a parody of spring,
Aped inmates? Patients here
Slept on hay and this afternoon

We queue like sheepish children
For the tablet trolley,
Candy counter that won't divert
The all-day double-honking donkey bray
Of Josie,
Without mind. Or is it
Meaning, is it
What we call gladness in the natural world
As the faint cry of those gulls
Dancing over the kitchen pickings:

A wheeling above
The leavings, mirth
In what she might have been?

8

Pat threw herself away
From babies, from
A seventh floor. Foetus-coiled
She sleeps all day
On two sun-coloured plastic chairs,
Snug by the mother-warmth
Of the radiator.

9

Reg was a Ship's Officer,
Blue Funnel, Ellermans.

Alert on the bridge and likewise
Scholarly in the chartroom,

He wheeled great cargoes
Through the Southern seas.

Struck off the pool, he slumps
Blindly on the windowsill,

His head plunged into his arms
That are guiding nothing.

10

One sits fluttering, fluttering.
Poor, pale moth stuck through with a pin.

One seeks me out to whisper
Extraordinary confidences
Concerning the holy ghost
And a computer. One

Rages up and down the day room
Shouting, 'It's shite.' Everyone's right.

11

The evening canteen
Is where like minds meet.
Eruptions of senile fisticuffs,
Dancing and even
Love I've seen:

One childishly sprawled
On another's knee,
Sucked kisses with cigarettes
Endangering the endearments.

Behind a partition,
The healthful sane are playing badminton.
The shuttlecock soars to heaven like a searchlight,
Drifts to the earth like snow.

Our side
Has a stout Edwardian billiard table,
Permanently sheeted,
Reserved for the diversions of the dead.

12

Many streets in the hospital,
'The largest of any kind
In Europe' when it was built and many
Minds within the mind.

'The shifting population
Of a grid-iron city.'
Pathetic co-operations and courtesies,
Hunger and pity.

This is your holy mountain,
Your shallow grave.
When nothing's left this is what's left
To save.

Sonnet for Dick

My friend looked very beautiful propped on his pillows.
Gently downward tended his dreaming head,
His lean face washed as by underlight of willows
And everything right as rain except he was dead.
So brave in his dying, my friend both kind and clever,
And a useful Number Six who could whack it about.
I have described the man to whomsoever
The hell I've encountered, wandering in and out
Of gaps in the traffic and Hammersmith Irish boozers,
Crying, where and why did Dick Johnson go?
And none of the carloads and none of the boozer users,
Though full up with love and with camaraderie, know
More than us all-of-his-others, assembled to grieve
Dick who, brave as he lived things, took his leave.

A Pastoral Disappointment

Habitate the heart's allotment!
   Tuber-lonesome, earth your doubt
Where the mild potato flowers
   By the peaceful brussels sprout
And the sea-green vegetation
   Calmly washes in and out
     Of light and shade:
A bird sings on the handle of a spade.

Put your shoulder to the silence,
   Bend the buttock to the stoop
Of the creosoted tool-shed.
   See the sweet pea loop the loop
Up the trellis. In due season
   And due order dress the troop
     Of lettuce heads.
Command a rainfall to refresh the beds.

Peace is in the heart's allotment.
   Where the sun has pressed its thumbs,
Tamping down transplanted neighbours,
   Are no mansions, nor are slums,
But an even-handed empire
   Where impartial kindness comes
     To each green thing:
A cabbage white could be this kingdom's king.

But wait! Garrotted in the bindweed,
    Who is this strip-farmer dead?
Slugs exploring either nostril,
    Eye-bulbs bursting from his head?
Hell is in the heart's allotment,
    From the green veins gouting red
        And its flames
Leaping in the bonfire's funeral games.

Mulch him down and fork him over,
    Turn his body through the light
Into mould of under darkness
    Where a rooted appetite
Works an income from his liver,
    Builds a star upon his night.
        Nature's art
And hell's compose the compost of the heart.

Sea Missive

Dear Voice:
     I heard you reading the Shipping Forecast
Yesterday afternoon and enjoyed it
Even more than usual.
     My bark, I may say,
Is far from ship-shape, backing northotherwise,
Poor to appalling . . . good,

Therefore, to be airwave-worthy,
And navigate not by your pinpoints
But by your encouraging tone
Alone:

For I have no bearings at all in this cliff-high sea
And when I go down off Rockall or Malin
Or Dogger or Finisterre,
The giant salt boon of your presence there
Will more than compensate
Me among Nereids: lonely Poseidon
Will likewise lean and listen with a deep-sea stare
To his fan-mail crackling
In my hair.

P.S. I've never put to sea.
I live in a tower block in SE 23.

Moorhouse

Vaguely Australian rural North Kentish accents
Were still to be heard when I was a child
Before that music fell from the wires

And universal flatter South London took wing
Over the beechwoods, the downland lanes,
Brackened hillsides of fiddlehead ferns,

The flint in the chalk and the chalk in the clay-grey
Ploughland. By country bus-stops
After the war men singly stood,

A wiry crest on the regimental blazer,
The macintosh over the arm, the head
Brylcreemed or brilliantined on summer evenings,

Bound for pints of mild in the British Legion.
Kindly they were, as I recall,
These roll-up makers from deep scarred tins,

To me and my brother, two long-legged oddities,
Posh and animated and shy,
The boys who lived in the private school on the hill.

One thing we had in common was that we were poorish:
That and cricket. In the soap-box pavilion
Smelling of linseed oil and manhood,

My father said, 'Who are we playing next week?'
'Ideal, Ronnie.' 'I'm sure it is, Ivor,
But who are we playing?' Ide Hill was the answer

After more puzzled exchanges. A witless old man
Called Reg, still with thick black hair,
Cackled at the proceedings from the boundary,

Half in and half out of the trees. In their shade
Round-armed women in ample frocks
Made sandwiches. Behind them

The Austins 7 and 10 and the half-timbered shooting-brake
Clustered in the rutted copse. The field
Is wilderness now like the underbrush on the hillside

Where the lost balls nest forever, the pitch
(Much moss on it in its bouncing days
Over a bed of flint)

Sapped of all danger. I see my long-dead father
Pivot in thigh-high grass to hook
Hard and high into now where the ball dissolves

With the Kentish voices in their time of day.

Victorian Family Photograph

Here is the mother all boobed and bodicey
Who started the children upon their odyssey.

There sits the father stern as a rock
Who rules the world with his iron cock.

Those the two children white as mice
Who saw the ghost in the attic, twice.

And who are we to suppose this vignette
Not threaded with love like a string quartet?

Letter to Anna, Pregnant

When I consider
By the frozen river
How we two shall never
Down some of these days
Meet in loving
Upon the ungrieving
Bank in forgiving
New-made rays

Of April sunlight
When touch is leaf-light
And love is outright
And darkness done,
Then I remember
Times without number
The cold I shouldered
To block your sun.

And I apportion,
By this sad station
Where ice to the ocean
Flows downstream,
All blame attendant
To your correspondent,
Sorrow his tenant,
Drowned that dream.

The hawthorn crouches
In the black wind's clutches
And snags and scratches
The last of light
That is dying over
The winter river
That sails forever
On out of sight.

I'm sorry, darling,
I hope the unfurling
Bud in your sailing
Body may
Beyond shores woeful
Wake you joyful,
Wake you joyful
Some sweet day.

Short Afternoons

Who would suppose a dryad in a laburnum
Accusing over a privet hedge? Or the woman
Who asks me the way and stares deep in my eyes
As though reading an autocue in them?
But we have entered

The country of short afternoons where every angle
Is filled with intense implication. Brickwork is pertinent,
Sycamore leaves
The wind scrapes widdershins over the pavement
Are freighted with dangerous meaning, a world

At your two-timing feet and its secret truth on the tip
Of your tongue. In the sky
A vapour trail is a pipe-cleaner metamorphosing
Into a papery silver birch limb, changing
Into a spoilage into the lake of darkness,

Sun knowing sudden
Disgrace as it falls from the arms of the tree of heaven.
And then the silver,
Black and too purple
Frieze is under vindictive construction,

Wind in its element again
Of Chaos and old night. So faces
That dip after work into pubs on the Holloway Road
Are electrical, tripped
Into such sudden transparency,

Into such lit significance there is reason
To fear and cherish, to huddle and talk excitedly,
Naming each other's names, since faces
Are offered once only, says the wind,
And the singable circumstance is being alive.

How the Wild South East was Lost

For Robert Maclean

See, I was raised on the wild side, border country,
Kent 'n' Surrey, a spit from the county line,
An' they bring me up in a prep school over the canyon:
Weren't no irregular verb I couldn't call mine.

Them days, I seen oldtimers set in the ranch-house
(Talkin' 'bout J. 'Boy' Hobbs and Pat C. Hendren)
Blow a man clean away with a Greek optative,
Scripture test, or a sprig o' that rho-do-dendron.

Hard pedallin' country, stranger, flint 'n' chalkface,
Evergreen needles, acorns an' beechmast shells,
But atop that old lone pine you could squint clean over
To the dome o' the Chamber o' Commerce in Tunbridge Wells.

Yep, I was raised in them changeable weather conditions:
I seen 'em, afternoon of a sunny dawn,
Clack up the deck chairs, bolt for the back French windows
When they bin drinkin' that strong tea on the lawn.

In a cloud o' pipesmoke rollin' there over the canyon,
Book-larned me up that Minor Scholarship stuff:
Bent my back to that in-between innings light roller
And life weren't easy. And that's why I'm so tough.

George Herbert's Other Self in Africa

Thinking another way
   To tilt the prism,
I vowed to turn to light
   My tenebrism
   And serve not night
     But day.

Surely, I cried, the sieves
   Of love shake slow
But even. Love subsists
   Though pressed most low:
   As it exists,
     Forgives.

But my stern godlessness
   Rose through the sun,
Admonished me: Fat heart,
   So starving's fun?
   Whom have they art
     To bless?

Thereat my false thought froze,
   Seeing how plain
The field was where they died,
   How sealed their pain,
   And I replied,
     God knows.

The Sub-Song

For Richard Mabey

I thought it a piece of fancifulness
when first I heard it mentioned:

the sub-song of the wintering bird:

but no, it's a scientific
classification of sound, denoting

a drowsily territorial
foreshadow, rehearsal or update,

sung past the leafless tree
in a minor key.

With no particular
dedicatee.

Or recitative between arias,
summer and summer,

song of the slumbering, fixate
middle-comer.

I think I have caught the sub-song sounded
in various winter bars

by singletons with their beaks buried under

their shoulders, or in supermarkets,
wobbling alone a trolley,

with one wheel
out of true:

far from the buzzard's mew
or the squawk of hawk on wrist,

crying, I fly, I can sing, I am here, I exist,
perpetually,

but it might have been nothing, or there again,
might have been me.